Alcohol problem-solving:
A humanistic nursing approach

Alcohol problem-solving: A humanistic nursing approach

by
Jeanette Laird-Measures

APS Publishing
The Old School, Tollard Royal, Salisbury, Wiltshire, SP5 5PW
www.apspublishing.co.uk

British Library Cataloguing in Publication Data
A catalogue record for this book is available from the British Library

© APS Publishing 2004
ISBN 1 9038771 1 3

Printed in the United Kingdom by HSW Print, Clydach Vale, Tonypandy, Wales

CONTENTS

Acknowledgements

I would like to take this opportunity to thank the following people for their help and support in writing this book. In particular, I would like to mention Professor Hazel Watson (for that last minute oh-so-elusive reference), David Cooper (without whose support and friendship in the beginning I would probably not have gone ahead with the book), my colleagues Anton Randle and Moira Macleod, for being tolerant of my adrenaline rush at the end, Highland Primary Care NHS Trust for letting me use some of the new detox protocol (thanks, Dougie), my colleagues on the management committee of the Nursing Council on Alcohol for approving of my ideas, and Valery Marston, Publisher, for being tolerant of all those silly questions.

A special mention goes to my husband, Paul, and our three boys—sorry for hijacking the holidays, especially Easter, boys!

Foreword

Excessive alcohol consumption causes a huge range of health and social problems and their widespread consequences means that nurses working in all health care settings encounter individuals who experience alcohol-induced health and social problems. There is some evidence to suggest that opportunities to give advice to patients which could prevent an escalation of their drinking to a problematic level are sometimes missed because nurses find it difficult to broach the subject.

In this book, Jeanette Laird-Measures brings together theoretical and practical perspectives on nursing people whose drinking has implications for their health in order to shed new light on ways in which nursing interactions can be improved for both the individual and the nurse.

Throughout the book, we meet the real live people who inhabit the case studies. These case studies provide excellent exemplars of situations which face nurses and their patients every day in a whole range of settings. Here we get to know them as individuals. Indeed, nurses reading this text will no doubt recognise some of their own patients in the people who populate the pages. They may well also recognise themselves. This approach enables us—the readers—to reflect on our own practice. Having learned about alternative strategies and ways of working, these should in turn help us to enable our patients to find new ways of thinking about the issues that affect they way they behave and how people behave towards them.

I like Jeanette's suggestion that, 'The simpler the better is often the most appropriate guideline' (*Page 30*). Although she was commenting on the readability of information leaflets, this is a theme that pervades this very readable book. It has been said that we should, 'Write to express, not to impress.' (Gunning, 1968) This is indeed what Jeanette has done and it is a pleasure to read a book on nursing theory which is jargon-free and easily understood. It is a book to inform, stimulate thoughtful reflection, and to enjoy, so please do just that!

Professor Hazel Watson
Department of Nursing and Community Health
Glasgow Caledonian University

Preface

There have been many developments in the care of patients with alcohol problems. Likewise, there have been many developments in the field of nursing, and in particular in how nurses deliver care. All nursing is based on underlying theory, but an essential question that needs to be asked by any critical, enquiring nurse is 'how relevant is this theory to my practice?'

An old Gaelic proverb tells us '*Ruigidh an ro-ghiullachd air an ro-ghlalar*' (the best of nursing overcomes the worst disease). If the 'best of nursing' equates with expert practice, one expects certain key attributes to be demonstrated in the nursing setting, such as holistic practice knowledge. This is a concept central to the book, which looks at a wide cross-section of alcohol problems in different nurse-care situations, and at the theory underpinning nursing practice as it is delivered in those settings. It focuses on four distinct theoretical pathways that will be discussed and illustrated throughout the text:

- Firstly, on the Humanistic Nursing Theory developed by Paterson and Zderad (1988)[1], a theoretical framework that one might at first criticise for being abstract, with no objective criteria for evaluation, as this would be antithesis to the theory itself

- Secondly on Peplau's Model of Care (Peplau, 1988)[2], which again has had its critics because of the use of time it demands in patient care delivery, and because of the lack of guidance in documentation that Peplau failed to offer

- Thirdly, on Prochaska and DiClemente's[3] Transtheoretical Model of Change (1983), which is well debated by the profession and, overall, holds great utility for assessing a person's level of motivation to change

- Fourthly, on the concept of critical reflective practice as conducted by nurses using different methodologies, and its utility in helping practitioners draw out the theory underpinning their practice.

The book aims to demonstrate a practical approach to using these four constructs in a way that is consistent with the essence of caring and empowering. After the introduction, which is a broad overview of alcohol problems, *Chapter 1* discusses models and theories in detail. *Chapters 2–8* are concerned with identifying the different stages of change and identifying interventions appropriate to that stage. Each of these chapters works around two case studies, and identifies steps within the nurse-patient relationship that help the patient begin to

1   Paterson J, Zderad L (1988) *Humanistic Nursing*. Publication No 41-2218: i–iv; 1–129. National League for Nursing, New York
2   Peplau HE (1988) *Interpersonal Relations in Nursing*, 2nd edn. Macmillan, Basingstoke
3   Prochaska JO, DiClemente CC (1983) Transtheoretical therapy: Towards a more integrative model of change. *Psychother Theory Res Pract* **19**: 276–88

work through his/her problems. *Chapter 9* looks at the role of medication and other supports, and *Chapter 10* is a resource file.

Throughout the book, I have used the feminine convention for the term 'nurse'. This is to avoid the clumsiness of the 's/he' format and aids clarity. Also, I have used the term patient for those coming into contact with nurses who are receiving their care. I recognise that client is often used, especially in outpatient specialist settings. However, this book is aimed at a wide variety of nursing staff in different clinical areas, and the convention of patient is universal.

I have anonymised all of the members of staff mentioned throughout the book. The same is true of the patients in the case studies, all of whom I have come into contact with during 24 years of nursing in several different settings (and countries), some of whom I have nursed, others have been nursed by those I have supervised.

Introduction

There has been a huge recognition across the nursing field of the increasing incidence in alcohol-related problems. Whereas it is recognised that drinking small amounts of alcohol can have a beneficial health effect (Paton, 2000), in particular because of its protective abilities against death in ischaemic heart disease when taken in small quantities, alcohol consumption is costing the Scottish NHS £1 billion a year, and the NHS as a whole somewhere in the region of £3 billion (Scottish Executive, 2002). If the statistics are examined, they make worrying reading:

- Alcohol is costing health, social work and criminal justice more in direct finances than Alzheimer's disease, stroke, drug misuse and schizophrenia (Catalyst, 2001).

- Hazardous drinking, defined here as regular consumption of over 40g of pure ethanol (5 units) per day for men, or over 24g of pure ethanol (3 units) per day for women, is greatest among:
    - 16–24 year olds
    - males (three times greater than for women)
    - single or co-habiting (41% and 38% respectively, compared to 20% married)
    - those who are struggling with finances
    - those of white ethnic origin (Coulthard *et al*, 2002)

- In 1998 the UK population spent £26,805 million on buying alcohol (Brewer's Society, 1999). This does not include illegally imported alcohol, a problem for Customs and Excise with the ease of access across the international ferry ports

- Somewhere in the region of 20% of patients who attend primary health care are recognised to be excessive drinkers (Alcohol Concern, 2001)

- 35% of pedestrians involved in road accidents were shown to have alcohol levels of at least 100mg per 100ml in 1998 (Alcohol Concern, 1999; accessed at: www.alcoholconcern.org.uk on 02/04.03)

This list could be endless and the fact still remains: alcohol consumption is costing the NHS millions in care for alcohol-related problems. That care is offered across the board in clinical areas, from primary health to trauma areas, care of the elderly, mental health—in fact, wherever a patient who happens to have an alcohol problem comes into contact with a health care professional. Arthur (1998) suggested that that nurses are in a unique position to provide help for this group of people by offering early intervention. He goes on to suggest that there is a strategy open to health care workers to offer help to patients with alcohol-related problems, but nursing curricula are not yet meeting the needs to equip nurses to deliver. Watson (2000) concurs with this, suggesting that teaching the relationship between alcohol and health ought to be part of the entire curriculum. The Royal College of Physicians (RCP, 2001) have recommended that all health workers should have access to improved education on alcohol (in order to change attitudes towards patients who misuse alcohol).

Within the chapters of this book, we will meet patients who have many problems related to their drinking; they will have relationship problems, they will have seizures, they will have hallucinations, they will be on a formal warning at work. The focus will be on the nurses who are caring for these patients, who are reflecting on their practice and agonising over whether or not their patient information leaflets are up-to-date (*Chapter 2*), or their discomfort at suggesting that a patient 'only' drinks one bottle of vodka a day instead of two. Importantly, we will also encounter some of the tools of the trade: the drinking diaries, the decision charts, the mood charts and the craving diaries that hold great utility for nurses in any setting, who want to help their patients move towards change.

This book aims to support both the reader who encounters patients with an alcohol problem in a clinical area and aims to provide interventions appropriate to her patient's presentation, and the reader who may want to reflect more deeply on her nursing practice. It does not aim to suggest that any nurse can replace the specialist services, which offer a wide range of in-depth care and work towards behaviour change. But a patient attending his first appointment at such a service who has completed a drinking diary and maybe even a decision chart that the practice nurse has given him in advance has already started to work towards that goal of change.

Harmful or even chaotic alcohol misuse is known to cause a wide range of problems. In order to progress towards exploring the nature of these problems, it is important to clarify how alcohol is measured, and what constitutes unwise and hazardous drinking. When working with problem drinkers, the starting point is often to assess just how much our patients have actually been drinking; as we are about to see, the best case scenario is the patient who brings his/her labelled empties. That doesn't happen. In the real world, we have to rely on 'guesstimates' based on the following.

In the UK the 'standard drink' used by the public health departments as a measure on which to base both guidance and policy direction has been described as one unit. A single unit of alcohol refers to a portion of drink that contains eight grams of pure ethanol. There are, however, inherent difficulties for practitioners working with patients who have an alcohol problem, especially those who may well be actively drinking in a harmful way, as we will see in *Chapters 2* and *3*. Firstly, different wines have different strengths, as do different ales and different spirits, so it is becoming increasingly difficult for people to know how much alcohol they have consumed in a session. Secondly, people who are at the problematic stage of their drinking may have poor short-term memories and, therefore, not be able to remember how much they have consumed. Although many retailers and distributors within the industry are stating the number of units on the bottle, if one is drinking in a public house, it is rare to see the units written on the pumps. On average, one unit of alcohol is the equivalent of:

- half a pint of ordinary strength lager/cider/beer at 3.4% strength
- a single, 25ml measure of 40% proof spirit
- a small glass (125ml) of 9% wine.

If we look at some of the more common drinks as bought and consumed in bars, unit measurement becomes a maze:

- 125ml glass white wine   12% = 1.5 units
- 1 'Alcopop™', 330ml standard bottle   5% = 1.7 units

- 1 pint premium lager   5% = 2.8 units.

The Government's latest advice on what constitutes sensible drinking can be interpreted as 2–3 units a day or less for women, or 3–4 units a day or less for men, with two alcohol-free days a week. Advice for pregnant women is currently one or two units a week. The Department of Health (1995) have said that drinking above these levels will increase the risk of harm. There is argument that this advice has led to confusion, as it could lead to what appears to an increase in the weekly limits from previous guidelines, which advised 14 units for women and 21 units for men as the cut off point (British Medical Association, 1995). The UK Alcohol Forum supports the British Medical Association's views, and within this book the overall pattern will be working towards these levels or lower in those who want to continue to drink.

Broadly speaking and for the purpose of this chapter, the problems caused by excessive or unhealthy alcohol consumption are categorised into physical, psychological and sociological, and will now be explored to contextualise some of the situations that we will encounter in subsequent chapters.

Physical problems associated with excessive drinking (Saunders, 1991; Marshall, 1997)

Alcohol affects most parts of the body and has an unusually high capacity to cause systemic damage in chronic excessive drinkers. In addition to the direct effects of the chemical on the cells, there are additional complications associated with its disinhibitory nature, such as unwanted pregnancy and exposure to sexually transmitted diseases, and also risks associated with trauma. Women are more at risk of alcohol-related damage because they have a leaner body mass causing proportionally higher blood alcohol concentrations than men drinking the same amount (Saunders *et al*, 1981).

Gastroenterological disorders are often the first to manifest, usually in the form of mild gastritis after a period of excessive drinking. This then leads to gastric ulceration, caused by the effect of alcohol increasing the diffusion of the stomach's hydrochloric acid through the mucosa. Gastric bleeds may ensue and there is a risk of pancreatitis developing, which can lead to chronic pancreatic failure. Oesophageal carcinoma is strongly associated with heavy alcohol use, as is colo-rectal cancer (Garro and Leiber, 1990).

Alcoholic liver disease is one of the main complications that occurs with chronic excessive consumption, and may be seen in one of three forms:

- **Alcoholic hepatitis**: this relates to inflammation of the liver, often with associated jaundice. There are necrotic changes seen in the cells of the liver, frequently accompanied by acute right-sided abdominal pain. It can also be asymptomatic, more chronic, and is usually diagnosed when the patient is examined because the liver edge is palpable; also, there will be raised liver enzymes in the blood, with other indicators, such as macrocytosis or reduced platelet count (associated with **bone marrow** disorder: alcohol is a **bone marrow** toxin)

- **Cirrhosis**: this refers to a period of permanent change in the liver, which becomes fibrous and unyielding as a response to heavy sustained alcohol consumption.

Chronic pain may ensue, which often presents in the back. Again, the liver function deteriorates, and indicators of the potential development of cirrhosis are seen in raised liver enzymes, in particular AST (aspartate aminotransferase). Definitive diagnosis includes biopsy

- **Fatty liver**: this occurs as a metabolic response to increased alcohol consumption (i.e. a difficulty in breaking down and disposing of fatty acids) and resolves on abstinence for a minimum of two months.

Cardiovascular disease is another complication that may develop as a result of excessive alcohol consumption. In particular, alcohol may cause arrhythmias, such as atrial fibrillation, and tachycardia is associated with alcohol withdrawal. Hypertension has been seen as a consequence of chronic alcohol misuse, although in most instances the blood pressure does lower with abstinence. Because of the effect of alcohol on the bone marrow, there is an increased risk of stroke (cerebro-vascular accident) as a result of haemorrhage due to thrombocytopenia; conversely, thrombosis is also more common in those with increased alcohol consumption, leading to increased risk of both cerebral and cardiac thromboses. Cardiac myopathy is also seen in heavy drinkers, leading to oedema and ascites.

Endocrine dysfunction is also noted in chronic drinkers. Notably, a form of Cushing's disease is seen, which is demonstrated by obesity, bloated face and hypertension, and is distinguished from true Cushing's disease by blood profile of the glucocorticosteroid levels. Abstinence from alcohol prompts reversal. The sex hormones are affected, leading to sub-fertility in men and women, and to gonadal atrophy.

Musculo-skeletal disorders associated with alcohol misuse and these include: myopathy (both acute and chronic, leading to wasting), osteoporosis, and gout. Although all improve with abstinence, the myopathy may be permanent, and both gout and osteoporosis need treatment with medication, often for life.

Neurological disorders are often seen in patients who present with alcohol-related problems. Peripheral neuropathy causes loss of sensation in the hands and feet and may spread up towards the knees. It does improve with thiamine, but long-term improvement can take up to a year and there may be permanent damage. Thiamine plays an important function in nerve repair and should be available for all patients who present with any neurological problems. The role of thiamine is discussed further in *Chapter 9*. Alcohol withdrawal seizures are a risk for up to ten days after stopping drinking, but are more common in the first 48 hours.

Brain damage caused by problematic alcohol consumption can, to a certain degree, be categorised alongside the other neurological disorders above, as many are associated with the thiamine deficiency we have already seen and the withdrawal symptoms associated with immediate abstinence. However, there are some disorders of special note that fall more into the category of neuropsychiatric syndromes (Saunders, 1991):

- **Delirium tremens**: This is an acute withdrawal state, which has its onset in the withdrawal symptoms that we will encounter in further chapters (anxiety, sweating, tremor, loss of appetite, nausea). It then leads into an agitated state where the patient becomes disorientated and has hallucinations. These are predominantly of a visual and tactile nature, with patients often seeing small animals, such as rats, and even feeling 'insects' crawling on their skin. It is frequently associated with auditory hallucinations and the patient is seen in a state of absolute terror. His/her state of awareness is not constant and a clouding of consciousness is sometimes seen in which the patient relates to those around as if he/she were somewhere else. One patient found in this condition was taken to the hospital by the police; when they arrived in his bedroom with the doctor, he thought he was in the garden and that the police were standing in the flowerbeds that he had spent the Spring digging and planting. As the autonomic nervous system is in a state of high excitation, the patient has marked tremor and often develops a pyrexia. Treatment needs to be instigated at once, as it can lead to cardiovascular collapse with a mortality rate of 4.9 per cent (Cushman, 1987). This would involve intravenous thiamine, high doses of diazepam, fluid and electrolyte replacement and often an antipsychotic medication, such as haloperidol (Chick, 1989). Nursing care is very specific if this occurs. The patient is terrified and ill; a calm demeanour is extremely important to avoid further confusion and misinterpretation of stimuli. A side room is advisable, within sight of the nurses at all times until the patient is more aware. We will meet a patient in *Chapter 6* who experienced something similar, and hear the nursing staff's discussion and reflection on their practice

- **Alcoholic hallucinosos**: This is a state in which the patient has developed predominantly auditory hallucinations and often some delusions (false, fixed beliefs). It appears over a longer period than delirium tremens and at first does not appear to be related to alcohol consumption because there are often no other visible signs of withdrawal. It does appear to be a type of schizophrenia and, indeed, the initial treatment would be the same (ie. antipsychotic medication) but with the addition of thiamine, and the patient is strongly encouraged to aim for abstinence from alcohol

- **Wernicke's encephalopathy**: This is a very specific syndrome associated with acute withdrawals from alcohol and is caused by acute thiamine deficiency. If thiamine is not given immediately, it can lead to irreversible brain damage, which is then the chronic form of the disease known as Korsakoff's psychosis. With Wernicke's encephalopathy, patients typically have signs of delirium tremens, but in addition they have the following:
    - Nystagmus to lateral gaze (this is tested by asking patients to follow a pen held in front of their face with their eyes; if the eyes wobble in the socket when they look to the side, this is a positive sign. Most people have a small degree of nystagmus in some conditions, but this type is marked)
    - Ataxia—often described as a dapping gait; it is as if the patient cannot feel the floor with his/her feet and are having to make wide deliberate flat steps
    - Clouding of consciousness (as described above)
    - Opthalmoplegia (this occurs when the eyes appear to roll back independently of each other in their sockets.

- **Korsakoff's psychosis**: This is often seen as the end stage of Wernicke's and is associated with years of alcohol abuse leading to long-term cognitive impairment. Characteristically, the patient with this has apathy, disorientation, and poor short-term memory (similar to dementia), although this is under debate in the literature (Saunders, 1991); there is also evidence of frontal lobe damage

Foetal alcohol syndrome is a range of disabilities caused when the unborn child has been exposed to the mother's drinking. Diagnosis in the child is dependent on the following four features (Plant, 1997):

- Pre- and post-natal growth retardation
- Physical anomalies (in particular, children who have this tend to have a narrower upper lip which is set lower below the base of the nose than is the norm, and their noses appear broader because the eyes appear to be set further apart; they also have asymmetric ears and a shorter nose than is the norm)
- The mother has an identifiable alcohol problem
- There is evidence of central nervous system dysfunction with cognitive impairment, and motor co-ordination is impaired (in the hand-eye range).

Sociological and psychological problems associated with heavy drinking

Alcohol problems are far reaching and extend well beyond the physical impact on the body. Al-Anon UK estimate that for every person who is alcohol-dependent, four others in their circle will be affected by their drinking (Al-Anon UK, 1995). Orford (1997) suggests that family members themselves are at risk of physical and mental ill health as a consequence of living with a problem drinker; *Chapters 2* and *6* explore some of these issues in more detail within the case studies provided. They also focus on the unique needs of women with alcohol problems, and on the problem of children in a drinking household.

One major problem facing society is suicide, with over 4000 deaths in this country each year. Broken down, the figures for 1998 are as follows (Department of Health):

- England and Wales   3614
- Northern Ireland   253
- Scotland   596

It has been estimated that 15–25% of suicides occur in patients with alcohol dependence, which makes the risk of suicide in these groups 20 times higher than the average population (Gunnell and Frankel, 1994). Sixty-five percent of parasuicides (suicide attempts) were linked to excessive drinking (Department of Health, 1995).

Clearly, these statistics are disturbing, and it is suggested here that assessing mood and previous history is an essential component in a patient's pathway through the care maze in order to contribute to the early detection and prevention of suicide. Questions that will lead nurses into exploring this can easily be added to a screening tool for use in primary health care settings. Although nurses have, in the past, stated their concerns at their ability to include screening and intervention for patients with alcohol problems (Cooper, 1994), there are several simple screening tools available, examples of which are given in later chapters. Moreover, nurses are actively screening for post-natal depression in three specific areas: maternity services, family health settings (health visiting and family health nurses), and primary health care (practice nurses). As it is becoming commonplace to ask questions on how women are feeling, it is not difficult to repeat the questions in an albeit modified form when dealing with problem drinkers. If and when the nursing curriculum is addressed as suggested by Watson (2000) (see *Page xiii*), it is to be hoped that such screening will be commonplace.

Another problem that has become more apparent in recent years is the impact of alcohol on the elderly. As a social group, the elderly (over 65 years of age) are among the poorest groups in the UK, more likely to be bereaved, more likely to suffer from clinical depression, more likely to be geographically isolated, and more likely to have reduced mobility. If these factors alone are compounded by drinking above recommended levels, each will be made worse, because alcohol has been shown to:

- Be a depressant
- Cause falls
- Cost money.

More worryingly, with the onset of older age, physiological changes would pre-dispose drinkers to develop problems, in particular because of a reduced capacity to metabolise blood alcohol. They have a higher prevalence of cancers and arthritis, which need medication and, because their bodies cannot clear substances as well as a younger patient's, the impact of alcohol alongside their medication can precipitate further problems. When nursing older adults, care must be taken to ensure that leaflets and other information are written in a format that is easily read, in a larger typeface, and not on shiny paper (Mumford, 1997). This is a recognition that eyesight does deteriorate as people age.

Nurses are in an ideal position to address drinking in the with older people. Health visitors in the UK are routinely carrying out a health check in this age group and the practice nurse also offers routine health screening in most GP practices. A simple three or four item questionnaire, such as the CAGE questionnaire (Mayerfield *et al*, 1974: 1121), which is suitable for all age groups, takes less than 40 seconds to complete:

CAGE questionnaire

Alcohol dependence is likely if the patient gives two or more positive answers to the following questions:

- Have you ever felt you should **C**ut down on your drinking?
- Have people **A**nnoyed you by criticising your drinking?
- Have you ever felt bad or **G**uilty about your drinking?
- Have you ever had a drink first thing in the morning to steady your nerves or get rid of a hangover (**E**ye-opener)?

The combination of CAGE questionnaire, MCV and GGT activity will detect about 75% of people with an alcohol problem. One positive answer generates the provision of leaflets and information; two or more generates a specialist referral.

In many instances, excessive drinking leads to employment difficulties. Nor does this have to be as a result of long term, chronic alcohol misuse. It has been demonstrated that between four and ten standard units of alcohol can impair judgement and co-ordination (Godfrey, 1992), leading to accidents in the workplace. Employers are becoming increasingly aware of the role that alcohol misuse can play in sickness and absenteeism, and in productivity, and are developing workplace alcohol policies. Some cater for those with a recognised problem and are willing to allow time away for their workers to attend support sessions with their key worker. Others rely on their own occupational health nurses to deliver the support, and are likely to offer training to those nurses in alcohol related issues. When services consider their effectiveness at addressing barriers to accessing support, one key issue lays within their opening hours. Do they offer lunchtime sessions? Are they open in the evenings to allow workers to attend on their way home?

Housing needs are another issue high on the public agenda. Street homelessness is often cited as one of the visible problems in society, with particular locations in bigger cities renown for 'park bench drinkers'. Often, the less visible housing crises are the ones that impact more deeply on the health services. In *Chapter 8* we meet Joan, who is on the point of leaving a violent partner. Although in the phase of the nurse-patient relationship in which we meet her, no decision is made about her housing plans on discharge, the nurse is involved in finding resources for her that might lead to exploring housing options. Housing crises with problem drinkers occur for many reasons—debt, violence, poor housing conditions (due to poverty of choice related to drinking choices). Problem drinkers face eviction and discrimination issues, and housing policy back in the 1980s effectively precipitated much of the crisis we now face in the UK; the push towards home ownership from the rented sector caused housing shortages, and the economic 'crisis of affordability' led to an unprecedented level of repossessions (Harrison and Luck, 1996).

Housing needs are addressed in the nursing assessment tools in most clinical areas, but often do not allow very much scope for asking the nitty gritty questions that will help a patient to begin to address his/her difficulties. Asking what the layout of the home is and whether it has stairs is clearly essential if we are dealing with mobility problems. The questions that need to be explored with people who are drinking problematically include:

- are there any problems with your landlord or the neighbours
- do you have a secure tenancy
- are you in any rent or council tax arrears
- do you have any need for furnishings or equipment?

Initially, it may be difficult, especially for newly qualified nurses, to feel comfortable asking such probing questions. However, as the nurse/patient relationship develops, so does trust and an effective working alliance with the patient builds up. This can then lead to partnership working with other lead agencies, such as the social work department, housing agencies, Women's Aid, all of which can be important partners in care in dealing with this essential need.

Crime and alcohol have been linked in several different ways. The most obvious link tends to be with violence and public disorder offences, and with drink driving. In 1999, 19% of road traffic fatalities were alcohol-related (Scottish Executive, 2001), although drink driving accidents have been shown to be on the decline. The legal limit for driving in the UK is 80mg of alcohol per 100ml of blood. In Scotland in 2000, persons accused of homicide who were over the age of thirty were more likely to have been drinking alcohol (67%) (Scottish Executive, 2000). Again, when carrying out an assessment, one area for discussion is criminality as, due to the chaotic nature of some people's drinking, their offending history could be compounded by failure to pay fines, leading to more trouble with the courts. If someone has outstanding fines or is due a court appearance, there is the possibility of partnership working within the criminal justice system and with the social work department, in order to begin dealing at a practical level with some of the problems.

One further problem that appears to be escalating is alcohol consumption in the young. In 1998, 24% of young women and 43% of young men in Scotland (aged 16–24) were drinking in excess of recommended limits, showing a dramatic increase from the 18% and 37% of 1995 (Scottish Health Survey, 1998). Whereas adolescence is the time for experimentation and boundary testing, it is also the time for increased peer pressure; sadly, young people who chose to drink self-report a high incidence of problems, such as unwanted sexual practices and reduced performance at school (or work) (Ahlström *et al*, 1997). The school nurse is the most likely health professional to meet this group of individuals, and the family planning nurse. Both are in a position to offer a brief intervention following one of a number of assessment tools, such as the CAGE questions we saw earlier.

Summary

Watson (2000) suggests that nurses are ideally placed to offer brief information and advice aimed at reducing alcohol-related harm. We have seen throughout this introduction the type of problems associated with alcohol, and the harm that results from excessive consumption. We have also started to recognise an indication of the role that nurses can play in some of the sociological problems, and in some of the screening activities available in their everyday settings (eg. over 75 screening, routing post-natal screening).

The following chapter will now explore the models and philosophy that will guide nurses in their practice in the situations that we encounter throughout the rest of the book. It also sets the scene for helping nurses to reflect on their practice and explore their own skills in offering interventions to problem drinkers and, in some instances, for highlighting their own learning needs.

References

Ahlström S, Haavisto K, Tuovinen EL (1997) Finnish country report for the European school survey project on alcohol and drugs (ESPAD); Themes no 1/1997. Helsinki: Stakes. In: Ahlström S (2000) The Young Adult. In: Cooper DB (2000) *Alcohol Use*. Radcliffe Medical Press. Abingdon

Al-Anon Family Groups (UK) (1995) *How Al-Anon Works*. Alanon UK, London

Alcohol Concern (1999) *Drink Walk Christmas Warning to Pedestrians*. Press release 16th December 1999. Accessed: http://www.alcoholconcern.org.uk/servlets/doc/173

Arthur D (1998) Alcohol-related problems: a critical review of the literature and directions in nurse education. *Nurse Educ Today* **18**: 477–87

Brewers' Society (1999) Statistical Handbook. Brewers Society, London

British Medical Association (1995) *Guidelines on Sensible Drinking*. BMA, London

Catalyst Health Economics Consultants (2001) *Alcohol Misuse in Scotland: Trends and Costs*. Scottish Executive, Edinburgh

Chick J (1989) Delirium tremens. *Br Med J* **298**: 3–4

Cooper DB (1994) Problem-drinking: alcohol survey results. *Nurs Times* **90**(14): 36–38

Coulthard M, Farrell M, Singleton N, Meltzer H (2002) *Tobacco, Alcohol and Drug Use and Mental Health*. The Stationary Office, London

Cushman P (1987) Delirium tremens: update on al old disorder. *Postgrad Med* **82**: 117–22

Department of Health (1995) *Sensible Drinking: The Report of an Inter-Departmental Working Group*. HMSO, London

Garro AJ, Leiber CS (1990) Alcohol and cancer. *Ann Rev Pharmacol Toxicol* **30**: 219–49

Godfrey C (1992) Alcohol in the workplace—a costly problem. In: *Alcoholism*. Centre for Health Economics, University of York, York

Gunnell D, Frankel S (1994) Prevention of suicide: aspirations and evidence. *Br Med J* 308:

Harrison L, Luck H (1996) Drinking and homelessness in the UK. In: Harrison L, ed.) *Alcohol Problems in the Community*. Routledge, London

Marshall EJ (1997) The clinical consequences of alcohol. In: Chick J, Godfrey C, Hore B, Marshall EJ, Peters T eds. *Alcohol Dependence: A Clinical Problem*. Mosby-Wolfe, London

Mayfield D, Macleod G, Hall P (1974) The CAGE questionnaire: validation of a new alcoholism screening instrument. *Am J Psychiatry* **131**: 1121–23

Mumford M (1997) A descriptive study of the readability of patient information leaflets. *J Adv Nurs* **26**(5): 985–91

Paton A (2000) The body and it's health. In: Cooper D, ed. *Alcohol Use*. Radcliffe Medical Press, Abingdon

Plant M (1997) *Women and Alcohol—Contemporary and Historical Perspectives*. Free Association Books, London

RCP (2001) Working Party of the Royal College of Physicians. *Alcohol—can the NHS afford it? Recommendations for a Coherent Alcohol Strategy for Hospitals*. Royal College of Physicians, London

Saunders JB (1991) Physical complications of alcohol abuse. In: Glass IB, ed. *The International Handbook of Addiction Behaviour*. Routledge, London

Saunders JB, Davis M, Williams R (1981) Do women develop alcoholic liver disease more readily than men? *Br Med J* **282**: 1140–3

Scottish Executive (2002) *Plan for Action on Alcohol Problems*. Alcohol Action Team Publication, Edinburgh: accessed at: *www.scotland.gov.uk/health/alcoholproblems*

Scottish Executive (2001) *Homicide in Scotland 2000*. Scottish Executive, Edinburgh

Scottish Executive (2000) *Road Accidents in Scotland 2000*. Scottish Executive, Edinburgh

Scottish Health Survey (1998) *The Scottish Health Survey*. HMSO, Edinburgh: Accessed at: *www.scotland.gov.uk/health/alcoholproblems*

Watson HE (2000) Prevention, information, education, and health promotion. In: Cooper DB, ed. *Alcohol Use*. Radcliffe Medical Press, Abingdon

1
Models and theories of nursing practice

This chapter outlines the humanist paradigm as the philosophy underpinning the book, and will suggest Peplau (1988) and Paterson and Zderad (1988) as nurse theorists from whom its philosophy is drawn and subsequent nursing care is delivered. It will also give a broad discussion of Prochaska and DiClemente's Model of Change (1983) and its continued use within health care settings as a means of assessing progress in patients with alcohol problems.

At the end of this chapter, the reader will have a greater understanding of:

- Nursing theory and its application to care delivery with problem drinkers
- Reflective practice as a method of increasing one's awareness of the knowledge underpinning practice
- Motivational interviewing and other techniques and skills
- The model of change.

Some thoughts on nursing and theory

Nurses have developed some shared views about the way that we assess our clients, the way that we plan, implement and evaluate their care, and on which we interact (Meleis, 1997). There is also an emphasis on basing all clinical decisions on evidence that demonstrates its efficacy (Department of Health, 1991). There is a host of research available to nurses with clinical interest in a diversity of areas, and nurses have access to many journals that may inform and guide practice. However, Thomson (1998) suggests that there is more to placing research firmly in the realms of practice than choosing what appears to be a valid intervention, as described in the literature, and hoping for the best. It is essential, for instance, that evidence gathered is rigorous, and the design and methodology is supported consistently by the stated research paradigm.

When exploring the research design of any study intended to be used to inform practice, a good place to start is by examining its methodology and research paradigm. Kuhn (1970) first introduced the concept of paradigms to a scientific community interested in the philosophical analysis of disciplines and their development. He eventually defined paradigms in the format by which they have now been adopted by the nursing community as: 'those aspects of a discipline that are shared by its scientific community' and went on to include the shared commitments and shared problems and solutions of that community.

This concept can be extended to include domains. The domain of nursing is the perspective and territory of the discipline (Meleis, 1997) and includes the subject matter of nursing, the agreed-upon values and beliefs, and all the individuals involved in the process (for example; the theorists, clinicians, researchers, and nurse tutors). In short, the domain of nursing describes both what nursing is and what nurses do. As for the former, Chinn and Kramer (1995) suggest that nursing includes caring, interaction, helping, supporting, enabling, and health promotion. The latter is often more difficult to conceptualise, as nurses 'do' different things in different settings.

Rose and Marks-Maran (1997) argue that whatever nurses 'do' (or the being and doing of nursing) includes intuitive, caring practice, and they go on to suggest that these actions are at the core of nursing scholarship, which they define as having the following components:

- critical thinking and practice
- reflective thinking and practice
- moral thinking and practice
- creative thinking and practice
- doing, knowledgeably and wisely
- caring
- intuitive thinking and practice
- being in a relationship with patients.

Two of these areas of nursing scholarship—critical and reflective thinking—are now proposed as essential components in reflective practice and, as such, are used to illustrate in each of the subsequent chapters of this book how nurses may explore their practice and highlight the learning that takes place on a daily basis. Schön (1987) describes how nurses use reflection-in-action to influence the care given:

> 'Often we cannot say what it is that we know. When we try to describe it we find ourselves at a loss, or we produce descriptions that are obviously inappropriate. Our knowledge is ordinarily tacit, implicit in our patterns of action and in our feel for the stuff with which we are dealing. It seems right to say that our knowing is in our action.'

This is not dissimilar to the ideas that Benner (1984) proposed with regards to intuition and expert nursing practice. She described this as understanding without rationale, and went on to outline how expert nurses are often unable to articulate their knowledge in action, but their experience and learning have become embedded into their practice. English (1993) criticises this theory, saying that intuition is by its very nature subjective, and that nurses must be able to validate their practice if the discipline of nursing is to further its research base to support its actions. One technique that nurses could adopt to explore the knowledge embedded into their practice is reflective discussion with either peers or a supervisor. Usually, a particular incident is discussed; for example, a meeting with a patient as part of care planning. Using an essentially catalytic process, the nurse is encouraged to reflect on an aspect of his/her work during the meeting, leading to critical analysis of the situation and the development of a new perspective. Thus learning is the ultimate outcome (Greenwood, 1993).

Atkins and Murphy (1993) suggest that skills for reflection on practice are as follows (for the purpose of illustration, the example of a session with a patient to discuss care planning is used):

- *Self-awareness*: this has to involve an honest examination by the nurse of her role within the care planning meeting (how she contributed) and how she felt about it (how she was affected)

- *Description*: this involves the nurse giving a thorough account of the situation (care planning meeting), recalling salient incidents and features

- *Critical analysis*: this involves the nurse examining the key components of the meeting, identifying existing knowledge about care planning, and challenging assumptions either about the process of care planning, or indeed about the patient's problems

- *Synthesis*: this is the integration of new knowledge with previous knowledge. In this example, the outcome of the reflective discussion will involve the development of a new perspective on either the process of care planning or the patient's problems, or some other aspect of the process

- *Evaluation*: this is the ability to make judgements about the value of something; in this instance, the care planning process. Does it need to change? Would a different model of care have been more appropriate?

How reflective practice sessions are conducted would depend entirely on the situation of each nurse. However, clinical supervision is one medium that incorporates reflection, and is becoming more available for most nurses. Indeed, the Department of Health (1993) and the United Kingdom Central Council for Nursing (1995) both recommended it be available, with the majority of nurses considering supervision to be an integral part of practice. Johns and Graham (1996) describe a model of reflective practice ideally suited to clinical supervision that has worked in many clinical settings, and which is relatively easy to establish as the norm because it relies on nurses bringing their own practice examples to the setting.

Reflective practice meets Paterson and Zderad, and Peplau's model

Within the practice examples presented in subsequent chapters, the reflective practice sessions are taken from clinical supervision held on a one-to-one basis between nurses and either their line managers or the clinical nurse specialist, or from group reflective practice sessions. It also includes reflective journal entries. In the given examples, the reflection and the care given has been facilitated from within a framework using Peplau's Model (Peplau, 1988) as the frame of reference. All the examples are based on real patients, nursed over a period of some 24 years, and real nurses, but the examples have been anonymised to protect confidentiality. Although small excerpts are given in each chapter, the following structure was used for the whole process in each instance, giving the four phases of the relationship between supervisor and supervisee that mirror the relationship between patient and nurse:

1. **Setting the scene; *Orientation phase***. The nurse shares general caseload and workload issues that have arisen since the last session. This does not include management issues,

which are dealt with in separate sessions. It is expected that a critical incident recording of one situation from the clinical area will have been made prior to the session;

2. **Telling the story;** *Identification phase*. The nurse describes the circumstances surrounding the clinical example and discusses the event, drawing out specific issues. The critical incident recording is used as a focus for some of the story telling;

3. **Facilitated reflection**; *Exploitation phase*. Here the supervisor uses a range of helping skills to guide the nurse into exploring the knowledge implicit in the nursing practice;

4. **Evaluation;** *Resolution phase*. Here the nurse summarises the main outcomes of her reflective discussion, which in most circumstances is an acknowledgement of the learning that has taken place. Often this involves the nurse setting further objectives.

Within the examples used in each chapter, the case studies are effectively the 'Telling the Story', as the full transcript of the sessions would be impractical to include here, and the subsequent narrative is part of the facilitated reflection. The examples are written verbatim, as they were recorded, hence the language used is at times colloquial.

Peplau's model holds as its focus the nurse-patient relationship (Peplau, 1988: 16), and says that its establishment is essential to the success of a patient's contact in his/her health care journey. The development of the nurse-patient relationship within the model has been depicted in *Figure 1.1* (after Simpson (1991) (see *Page 5*)

This is adapts well for use in supervision settings, as it is essentially about two people meeting and working collectively on problems to achieve resolution. In order to understand the model in action as presented in the subsequent chapters, it is important to look at some of the concepts that underpin its theory. Firstly, nursing is described as a 'significant, therapeutic, interpersonal process' (Peplau, 1988). As with other interactionist theorists, Peplau describes the goal of nursing as being related to assisting patients to find meaning; specifically, nursing is seen as the forward movement of personality and other ongoing human processes in the direction of creative, constructive, productive personal and community living. Clinical supervision mirrors this process, as the supervisor and supervisee work towards creative solutions to potential problems within the work role and, at the same time, part of the role of supervisor is to facilitate the supervisee to develop personal strengths. In order to achieve the goal of nursing, Peplau suggests that within the nurse-patient relationship both parties have roles to play. The nurse may be educator or health promoter for instance. This is particularly relevant for patients with an alcohol-related problem, as the key to change in many instances is balanced, reliable information on which patients can base a decision.

When one explores the roles that patients play within the nurse-patient relationship, it is important to consider that the nurse and the patient may well have different expectations of each other. If a role is a set of norms that dictate behaviour in a given situation, then in a medical setting where patients are expected to be in bed receiving care, it is possible that the patient will respond by adopting the 'sick role'. This is traditionally seen as passive, subservient (Stockwell, 1972). Clearly, this is not ideal if we are expecting patients to make active change decisions and take responsibility for their drinking behaviour. However, it is possible to challenge these assumptions when offering treatment in different settings and Peplau's model, in line with other interactionist approaches, is an ideal method of delivering care because it allows patients to find meaning in their situation rather than relying on merely doing and functioning. For example, as will be discussed in later chapters,

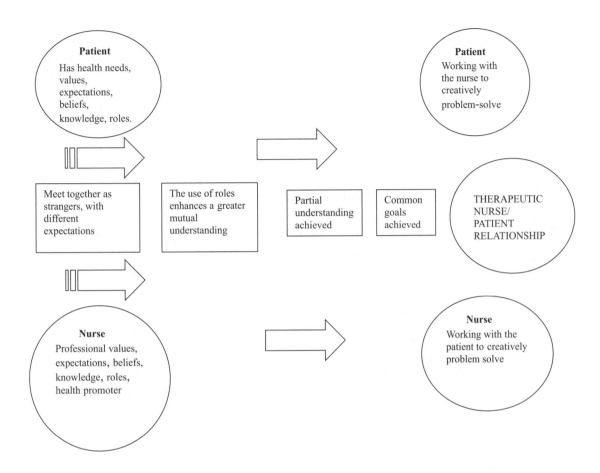

Figure 1.1: Nurse-patient relationship

detoxification in general ward settings will be more successful if the patient is encouraged to use the day room and be out of bed during the day. Rollnick and MacEwan (Davidson *et al*, 1991) point out that patients in general medical settings are often there because of other problems, and are not always willing to discuss their drinking, especially given the tendency for medical staff to use terms like alcoholic. If patients are encouraged to normalise as much as possible within the clinical setting, they are able to take on a more equal role within the nurse-patient relationship and, therefore, are more likely to address some of the more difficult issues. This is one benefit of using a developmental or interactionist model of care over a systems-based model within the clinical area. The focus is not on the body and its functioning or the 'disease of alcoholism', but on how the patient can work collaboratively with the nursing staff to achieve well being. The focus is to a large extent on the relationship between the patient and the care-giver.

This concept of normalisation in patients within medical settings is addressed if the question of roles is explored further and, in particular, within a humanist paradigm. Paterson and Zderad (1988) set out a theory of nursing that sits comfortably in the same interactionist framework as Peplau's model. They proposed that the nurse and the patient are both significant components in the nurse-patient situation, and that they each have experiences that influence the nursing process. Importantly, in setting out their assumptions about nursing, they say that 'Human beings are free and are expected to be involved in their own care and in decisions involving them'. This challenges the assumption that patients have a tendency to engage in sick role behaviour within the general ward environment and would appear to be a valid mantra for all nurse-patient encounters; it also sits comfortably with the clinical supervision process.

When compared, *Table 1.1* shows the major nursing concepts of the two models according to Meleis (1997).

Table 1.1: Peplau v Paterson and Zderad—theories compared

Concept	Peplau's Model of Nursing	Paterson and Zderad
Nursing	Nursing is a significant, therapeutic, interpersonal process.	Nursing is a human dialogue, a presence of both patient and nurse.
Goals of Nursing	The forward movement of personality and other ongoing human processes in the direction of creative, constructive, productive personal and community living	The development of human potential and more well-being for both the patient and the nurse.
Nursing therapeutics	The development of problem solving skills through the interpersonal process.	Humanness—in other words, the use of self, existentially nurturing, being, relating, meeting, and maximum participation.

Critique of the models

Both models have much to offer nurses in all settings who come into contact with patients that drink excessive amounts of alcohol because of their focus on the therapeutics of the nurse-patient relationship. They de-medicalise alcohol problems and instead help patients to develop their own ability to tackle problems. However, it is important to recognise that nurses trying to use a humanist approach to care will come across some problems with both models, although none are insurmountable.

Peplau's model relies on both the nurse and the patient being equal partners in care. As will be seen later on in this chapter, those patients in the pre-contemplation stage of change are reluctant to accept their alcohol consumption as problematic, which feeds into the anxiety of their situation. The axiology of Peplau's model is essentially psychoanalytical; she developed the model from an early attempt to explore how nurses do what they do (Peplau, 1988). In order for this to happen, there has to be an understanding on the part of the nurse of the anxiety experienced by the patient in the care setting, for that patient or their carer to begin to understand the nature of his/her problems, and to develop effective coping skills. Herein lies a problem if nurses are working in settings where they themselves have no access to clinical supervision, or adequate support.

An early study by Menzies (1970) showed how hospital social systems function as a defence against anxiety. For instance, nurses in difficult clinical areas have the ability to 'hide behind their uniform' to reduce the stress of dealing with dying patients. Nurses using a humanist approach to care need to work in an empathic way in order to engage with the anxiety evident within the nurse-patient relationship. In other words, in order to adopt a humanist nursing model, the nurse is working in a way that has essentially been socialised out of her own working experience. Simpson (1991) argues that, when nurses learn to use the anxiety experienced by the patient or carer to help them to understand the nature of the problems, they are effectively empathising with them. This empathy helps both the patient and the nurse to learn and grow. However, empathic understanding involves the nurse experiencing with the patient and, unless supported, this can lead to nurses feeling vulnerable. A clinical supervision policy that is adhered to and given priority would help to address some of those anxieties, as the nurse would be able to work in the certainty that she can take critical incident recordings along for discussion within a supportive, learning environment. This is an example of one such policy developed by a community mental health team:

Clinical supervision will be an empowering process for the supervisee that reflects our delivery of care. Supervision will take place a minimum of once every calendar month, for a two-hour session. This period is negotiable between supervisor and supervisee.

Supervisee:

- Brings the agenda
- Sets the time
- Sets the date
- Sets the venue
- Keeps the notes
- Brings any case notes for auditing, whether discussing pressing or long-term cases
- Brings a critical incident recording

Supervisor:

- Facilitates the session using Johns' model of reflective practice (Johns and Graham, 1996)
- Ensures that notes and conversation remain confidential to the supervision session. However, should issues arise which the supervisor or supervisee consider necessary to address elsewhere, then proposed action will be agreed upon and recorded within the session.
- The supervisor will not use supervision for disciplinary purposes or management supervision

The process of supervision will involve reflection on practice to facilitate learning. It will include clinical and personal development elements. Supervision of the caseload will be a salient feature, and an agreement will be reached between supervisor and supervisee on how to ensure that all cases are reviewed over a suitable period of time

---

Figure 1.2: Clinical supervision policy

It must be noted that, for adequate supervision to be offered, this raises a training issue. It is not enough for staff to be supervised by their line manager merely because of their position in the hierarchy. It would be more appropriate to offer peer supervision if the nurse's peer has had more training and experience.

One of the essential aspects of using a humanist approach to care is offering the patient time. This again raises an issue if caseloads are high, when there are staff shortages or other similar pressures. In these circumstances, it becomes a quality issue as it could be argued that time spent with the patient is a healing process and is the essence of nursing care. However, it is difficult to build up a relationship with a patient in short stay situations; i.e. day care or 24-hour admission situations. In these settings, whatever the model used for care, it is possible to adopt salient humanist features for care delivery. Paterson and Zderad (1976) proposed that every encounter with another human being is an open and profound one, with a great deal of intimacy that deeply and humanistically influences. Thus, in a setting where the CPN is the key worker in the community, but the patient comes into hospital for 24-hours observation after excessive vomiting, the nursing care, if delivered from a humanistic framework, will be meaningful and could help support his change decisions.

Another criticism of the humanistic model of nursing relates to the dilemma that it poses for nurses with regards to suffering. The alleviation of suffering has long been regarded as a role of nursing, but within the humanistic model the patient is encouraged to experience and learn from the suffering. The proposal within this book addresses the core of such a dilemma: that nurses adopt humanistic principles, assumptions and paradigmatic propositions in their delivery of care through the practical framework of Peplau's model. Within Peplau, it is the role of surrogate and teacher adopted by the nurse in a nurse-patient relationship that helps the patient achieve the humanistic principle of learning from and growing as a result of the experience of suffering, and its focus on creative problem-solving would lead to the suffering being addressed and alleviated as a priority.

Prochaska and DiClemente's Model of Change

When we consider patients who present with an alcohol problem, it soon becomes clear that different interventions will ultimately be more appropriate for individuals within each setting, and within the individual's unique circumstances and frame of reference. However, a key issue to be explored is that of their readiness to change in relation to the nature of their problematic behaviour. Prochaska and DiClemente (1983) developed a useful method of determining a client's stage of change in their addictive behaviour. The model can be represented as in *Figure 1.2 (Page 9)* and will be used as a basis for assessment and care planning.

In the pre-contemplation stage of change, patients present as having no fixed awareness that their drinking is causing problems and in some situations this has led to their help-seeking behaviour. It may be for instance that the man admitted via Accident and Emergency on a Monday morning, having had an alcohol withdrawal fit, knows well that problematic drinking is causative in the development of his dependency and withdrawal symptoms and, ultimately, the seizure. However, if in pre-contemplation, he is at a stage where he is unready to ask for help or make changes. Tober (1991: 21) argues that the drinking will be seen as a solution not the problem in those who come to regard their drinking as fulfilling needs. In this example, he may choose to continue drinking to prevent withdrawals and seizures, rather than seek help, such as detoxification and anti-epileptic medication.

It is often discouraging to nurses working with problematic drinkers in the pre-contemplation stage of change; in some settings, the same patients being admitted time and time

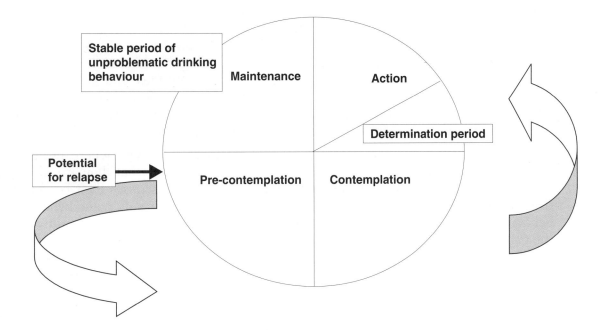

Figure 1.3: Model of Change (Prochaska *et al*, 1992)

again with the same problems can lead to nurses questioning the efficacy of helping. These questions are useful markers for staff to consider exactly what is being offered, and whether what is offered is appropriate for this, ultimately, challenging stage of change. Debating the efficacy, for instance, of offering to detoxify a patient who doesn't want to stop drinking is a useful reminder to us of the often impossible situation in which staff in acute settings are placed. In the first instance, harm minimisation is the most appropriate therapeutic intervention to offer, as this enters the patient's frame of reference by acknowledging his/her unwillingness to make big changes. This will be discussed further and demonstrated using case studies and care plan examples in *Chapters 2* and *3*.

The contemplation stage of change is characterised by patients recognising that they have a problem with their drinking, but have yet to make firm plans or commitment to change. Typically, these patients are showing signs of ambivalence and may be seeking new information on which to base their decision whether or not to change (Baldwin, 1991: 41). This is a time of discomfort for patients, who may be experiencing strong urges to drink in their typical pattern, while at the same time recognising the difficulties they are in, thus, leading to a distinct sense of indecision. The nursing challenge at this stage of change is to encourage patients to resolve their ambivalence for themselves by making a decision, and encouraging that decision to be one that promotes well-being. One method of working with patients at this level has been motivational interviewing (Miller and Rollnick, 1991), which is easily adaptable to most interaction situations between nurses and their patients.

In motivational interviewing, the therapist (nurse) recognises that clients (patients) are experts in their own drinking. The intention is to use that expertise in helping them to make changes for themselves by encouraging them to make self-motivational statements. Miller and Rollnick (1991) discuss five principles of motivational interviewing, which, when married with a humanistic nursing approach for use in nursing settings, may be seen as follows:

1. *Expressing empathy*. This is essential in helping patients to see that their nurse is understanding of their problematic drinking and personal situation and is, therefore, not going to be judgmental or authoritarian. Paterson and Zderad (1988) talk about nursing's 'existential involvement in patient care' being manifested in the active presence of the nurse. Valle (1981) found that the attitudes and interpersonal functioning of alcoholism counsellors directly influenced client outcome. Thus, in the orientation phase of the nursing process, as in the other phases, the nurse's use of empathy is a pre-requisite for the initiation of motivational work;

2. *Develop discrepancy*. This refers to a stage in motivational interviewing where the nurse gently raises patients' awareness of the incongruence between what they are saying about their drinking behaviour and what they are doing. This raises their cognitive dissonance, a state of internal tension that arises when a person's values and beliefs, or behaviour, disagree with one another (Festinger 1964). When this happens, it motivates the patient towards a motivational choice. This is consistent with humanistic nursing, which assumes that human beings have an innate force that moves them to know their angular views (Paterson and Zderad, 1988); the process of developing discrepancy helps to raise patients' awareness of their own role within their healing potential;

3. *Avoid argumentation*. This principle guides the nurse and the patient into keeping resistance to a minimum. When confrontation arises, values and opinions are likely to become entrenched and polarised, and the internal dissonance becomes unbearable; thus, the patient is more likely to choose previous behaviour (chaotic drinking) as a means of resolving the dissonance because it is a known and trusted coping mechanism. Within a humanistic nursing framework, it is expected that the goal of well being will be enhanced by the nurse and the patient as they experience the process of making choices together—and although there will be some conflict in goals during this crucial stage of motivational interviewing, a supportive, open relationship between the two will prevent this being an obstacle to change;

4. *Roll with resistance*. This is the principle within motivational interviewing that allows patients to decide whether or not to accept or reject what the nurse is suggesting. If the nurse is focussed on her attitude being 'right' because of her own knowledge, skills and experience, then patients are likely to feel patronised. It is crucial for patients to recognise their expertise in their own drinking for them to feel comfortable in accepting that there is a need to change;

5. *Support self-efficacy*. This is the principle by which nurses help patients to believe that they can be responsible for their own behaviour change and, more importantly perhaps, that they have the ability to carry it through. This is more likely to develop where there is a mutuality within the nurse-patient relationship (Paterson and Zderad, 1988).

In terms of the mechanics of carrying out motivational interviewing, the nurse will offer several motivational tools aimed at raising the patient's awareness, such as a decision chart. This and other tools will be illustrated within the case studies in *Chapter 4* and to a certain extent in *Chapter 5*. However, the nursing skills involved are based on the following:

- **Asking open-ended questions**. These allow patients to reflect at their own pace, and prevent the nurse from inadvertently leading them along a line of discussion that may be outwith their own frame of reference

- **Listening in a reflective manner**. This involves active listening skills, such as re-stating a sentence that the patient has just said, but putting an inflection at the end to make it into a question. The effect of this is that the patient then repeats what he/she has said but expands upon it, thereby clarifying his/her own thoughts

- **Affirmation and summarising**. This involves restating what patients have said, but in a way that helps them to take stock within a session of what has been said and even decided upon before moving on. It gives patients a chance to clarify the nurse's understanding in case there are discrepancies

- **Eliciting self-motivational statements**. Here the nurse encourages her patients to make statements for themselves about their need and potential for change with regards to drinking behaviour. For example, she might say something like 'From your time-flow chart you clearly have an idea when your problem drinking times are. Can you show me the times when you drink less and are pleased by your progress?' This encourages her patients to reflect on their ability to change in a positive way.

At the end of the contemplation stage of change, the patient will either remain where he is, move back into pre-contemplation, or will move into a period of determination if he has made a positive choice. This is characterised by the patient knowing that he is ready to make some changes in his drinking behaviour, but not necessarily having a clear idea on what changes he would like to make, or how he will achieve those changes. One of the goals of humanistic nursing is as follows:

> 'To help patients and self to develop their human potential and to come toward, through choice and inter-subjectivity, well-being or more well-being. To help patients and self to increase the possibility of making responsible choices'

(Paterson and Zderad, 1988)

Within Prochaska and DiClemente's model of change, this period is seen as preparation for change, and is marked by the nurse facilitating the planning of such change by the patient. This is discussed further in *Chapter 5* and illustrated by two case studies.

The action stage of change is characterised by patients making the changes that they have carefully planned for with the help of the nurse and other care providers. Here we see detoxification, for instance, or the commencement of a controlled drinking programme. It is the period of intense activity usually associated with the exploitation phase of the nurse-patient relationship when using Peplau's model of care (Peplau, 1988), and is the period of being and doing within a lived dialogue in a humanistic framework. Again, this stage of the model is discussed in more detail within *Chapters 6* and *7*.

The maintenance stage of change poses its own unique difficulties for the nurse and her patients. Here patients are focussing on maintaining change decisions through their daily lives, and on re-arranging their daily living to accommodate such change in order to prevent relapse. On the one hand, it can be the most rewarding experience for the patients and their families to see the end of the suffering. One of the participant's in Smith's study (Smith, 1998: 220) said of previous drinking behaviour '..I wouldn't like to go back to it. I couldn't go through all that'. On the other it can be a daily struggle for some until their confidence in their own ability to maintain their change grows. This stage of change is discussed in detail in *Chapter 8*.

Summary

This chapter has been a roller coaster of models and theories of practice. It proposes the applicability of the humanistic model of nursing to clinical settings when delivered through the medium of Peplau's model, and highlights the model of change as an appropriate structure from within which the patient may be assessed and appropriate care and interventions delivered. The following chapters will now take each stage of change and demonstrate using care studies, reflective practice transcripts, and a range of therapeutic tools and methodologies describing the practicalities of delivering such care.

References

Atkins S, Murphy K (1993) Reflection: a review of the literature. *J Adv Nurs* **18**(8): 1188–92

Baldwin S (1991) Helping the unsure. In: Davidson R, Rollnick S, MacEwan I, eds. *Counselling Problem Drinkers*. Routledge, London

Benner P (1984) *From Novice to Expert: Excellence and Power in Clinical Nursing Practice*. Addison-Wesley, Menlo Park, CA

Chinn PL, Kramer MK (1995) *Theory and Nursing: A Systematic Approach*, 4th edn. CV Mosby, St Louis

Department of Health (1991) *Research for Health: A Research and Development Strategy for the NHS*. Department of Health, London

English I (1993) Intuition as a function of the expert nurse: a critique of Benner's novice to expert model. *J Adv Nurs* **18**(3): 387–93

Festinger L (1964) *Conflict, Decision and Dissonance*. Stanford University Press, Stanford

Greenwood J (1993) Reflective practice: a critique of the work of Argyris and Schön. *J Adv Nurs* **18**(8): 1183–87

Johns C, Graham J (1996) Using a reflective model of nursing and guided reflection. *Nurs Stand* **11**(2): 34–38

Meleis AI (1997) *Theoretical Nursing*, 3rd edn. Lippincott, Philadelphia

Menzies I (1970) *The Functioning of Social Systems as a Defence Against Anxiety*. Tavistock, London: (Pamphlet No 5)

Miller WR, Rollnick S (1991) *Motivational Interviewing: Preparing People to Change Addictive Behaviour*. Guildford Press, New York

Paterson J, Zderad L (1988) *Humanistic Nursing* (Publication No. 41-2218: i–iv; 1–129). National League for Nursing, New York: In: Meleis AI (1997)

Paterson J, Zderad L (1976) *Humanistic Nursing*. John Wiley and Sons, New York

Peplau HE (1988) *Interpersonal Relations in Nursing*, 2nd edn. Macmillan, Basingstoke

Prochaska JO, DiClemente CC, Norcross JC (1992) In search of how people change: applications to addictive behaviours. *Am Psycholog* **47**: 1102–14

Prochaska JO, DiClemente CC (1983) Transtheoretical therapy: towards a more integrative model of change. *Psychother Theory Res Pract* **19**: 276–88

Rose P, Marks-Maran D (1997) A new view of nursing: Turning the cube. In: Marks-Maran D, Rose P eds. *Reconstructing Nursing: Beyond Art and Science*. Ballière Tindall, London

Smith BA (1998) The problem drinker's lived experience of suffering: an exploration using hermeneutic phenomenology. *J Adv Nurs* **27**: 213–22

Stockwell F (1972) *The Unpopular Patient*. Royal College of Nursing, London

Thomson MA (1998) Closing the gap between nursing research and practice. *Evidence-Based Nurs* **January** : 1 1.

Tober G (1991) Helping the pre-contemplator. In: Davidson R, Rollnick S, MacEwan I, eds. *Counselling Problem Drinkers*. Routledge, London

Valle SK (1981) Interpersonal functioning of alcoholism counsellors and treatment outcome. *J Stud Alcohol* **42**: 783–90

2
Working with pre-contemplators 1:
Inpatient areas, general ward settings

Nursing pre-contemplative drinkers poses quite a challenge for staff in acute and general ward settings. The very nature of the stage of change is that patients are not yet ready to accept the extent of their difficulties, or move on from their current situation. Amy, a chemist shop assistant, had this to say of pre-contemplation after she had moved on in her thinking:

'I remember all the mouthwash I would buy. And I think I bought more make-up than I ever sold to cover my puffy eyes. It never worked, of course, just faded as the shift wore on, but I wouldn't worry because by then I'd topped up from my flask...'

The following chapter discusses some of the issues that occur for these patients, and their carers, and uses the example of a patient who is a drinker, and a patient who is the husband of a drinker. At the end of this chapter, the reader will have a greater understanding of:

- The pre-contemplation stage of change
- The type of information needed by patients' in this stage of change to help them begin to consider altering their lifestyle
- The needs of carers and their families
- Some women's issues.

* * * * *

Case Study I

The first patient that we meet in this often difficult stage of change is Colin, who has been in and out of this particular setting on many occasions:

Colin is a 29-year-old man who has been a regular occupant of the local police cell on a Friday night. He was brought into the acute medical admission ward from the police station following a with-drawal seizure during the night, having been arrested for drunk and disorderly conduct. On admission to the unit, he had been post-ictal: confused, agitated, with poor short-term memory and some sensory and perceptual disturbance. The admitting nurse had decided to monitor him closely during the night and had placed him in a room adjacent to the nursing office. Just prior to the morning shift coming on duty, she had been able to spend some time with him, and had asked him both how he was feeling and what he wanted to do. He made it clear that as soon as the bus service started, he would be going home and that he needed no help. She completed an AUDIT questionnaire with Colin and scored the result to share with him, and to include in his discharge letter to the GP.

The nurse gathered a small package of information together, including a resource directory of local alcohol services and some health promotion leaflets, then arranged for a thiamine prescription to be dispensed.

As can be seen from the above case study, Colin is at the pre-contemplation stage of change. He is demonstrating no desire to change his behaviour, neither is he demonstrating any ambivalence associated with the later contemplation stage. Moyers (2000: 152) describes how this stage is characterised by the patient being surprised or taken aback at the thought that his/her drinking needs to change.

It may be thought that there is little in the way of help that can be offered to this group of individuals as, if they are not able to recognise the reality of a problem, it may be assumed that there is no point in intervention. However, the opportunity for helping patients to explore and, therefore, confront their problem-drinking, with its associated suffering, presents itself each time such a patient comes into contact with the services—be it at the practice nurse's well man clinic, or in an acute medical ward. Smith (1998) found that the evocation of suffering within a safe, therapeutic relationship was a motivating strategy for problem-drinking; such a relationship is the focus of nursing using Peplau's model as already discussed in the previous chapter. Tober (1991: 21) challenges the view that effective interventions for this patient group are not available, and concludes that 'something can be done' (1991: 38).

The following is a transcript of part of a reflective practice session between the nurse and her supervisor that explores the development of a nurse-patient relationship between the nurse and Colin, highlighting some of the strategies available to nurses in similar situations.

* * * * *

Supervisor = S;   Nurse = N

S: So, he said he 'was fine'— what were his non-verbals telling you?

N: *Difficult to say, really, er .. his legs were a bit twitchy, oh, aye, when I asked how he was feeling he looked away when he answered ..*

S: Looked away?

N: *Aye, he looked away .. I got the feeling he didn't really want to think about it, really.*

S: What did you say then?

N: *[laughs] I cannae remember really. I remember saying something like 'so you feel fine, but you had a fit'. I think I wanted to show him that what he was saying and what he was doing just didnae add up. It's like, I remember reading once that if you point out the discrepancy between what someone says and what someone does then it raises their awareness. I think that's what I was trying to do .. You don't think it worked, do you?*

S: [laughs] I don't think you do.... So, the info(rmation) pack?

N: *Well, I figured that if he read it when he got home, something may well sink in. I gave him our telephone number as well, you know, the one for the ward. I know that if agencies are non-confrontational then folk are more likely to come back, so I thought that if we were just gentle with Colin, but at the same time let him know that we could help even if it was a limited way then it might encourage him to keep in touch.*

S: And the AUDIT tool?

N: *I wanted to let his GP see the result, because he could then perhaps use it when he saw Colin next to try to raise his awareness of the problem his drinking was causing. Colin seemed to be honest when he was completing it; in fact, I think he appreciated the time I took with him over it. I didn't think the impact of it all had hit him there and then, but who knows, when he got home he may well think back to our conversation before he picked up his next drink*

* * * * *

This case study and discussion between the nurse and her supervisor highlight one of the domain concepts of nursing, as described by Paterson and Zderad (1988):

• Nursing process: *'deliberate, conscious, responsible, aware, non-judgemental existence of the nurse in the nursing situation, followed by disciplined, authentic reflection and description'.*

Within the case study, we saw how the nurse offered Colin time to share how he was feeling and what he wanted to do. Even though he made it clear he was leaving as soon as the bus service started, she let him know by her actions that she was still willing to help. She provided him with a resource pack that he may choose to read at some stage in the future and at no stage made him feel that she was criticising his drinking behaviour. During the reflective practice session, she demonstrated her awareness of motivational interviewing techniques by using a gentle confrontation aimed at raising Colin's awareness of the effect his drinking was having on his well-being.

The AUDIT tool that the nurse completed with Colin is a standard questionnaire developed to give continuity to the assessment of the presence of alcohol problems. Murray (1992) suggests that the act of helping patients to fill in such a chart can in itself be an effective intervention, as it encourages them to reflect on their behaviour. By asking Colin to fill this in with her, the nurse was acting in the role of educator, as the scoring process at the end is structured in such a way that it gives direct feedback to the likelihood of a problem existing. A copy of the tool in its usual format is shown on *Page 18*.

ALCOHOL USE DISORDER IDENTIFICATION TEST (AUDIT)

(Saunders *et al*, 1993)

Please circle the answer that is correct for you

1. How often do you have a drink containing alcohol?

    Never   monthly or less   2–4 times a   2–3 times a   4 or more times a
                                        month   week   week

2. How many standard drinks containing alcohol do you have on a typical day when drinking?

    1 or 2   3 or 4   5 or 6   7 to 9   10 or more

3. How often do you have six or more drinks on one occasion?

    Never   less than monthly   monthly   weekly   daily or almost daily

4. How often during the last year have you found that you were not able to stop drinking once you had started?

    Never   less than monthly   monthly   weekly   daily or almost daily

5. How often during the last year have you failed to do what was normally expected from you because of drinking?

    Never   less than monthly   monthly   weekly   daily or almost daily

6. How often during the last year have you needed a drink in the morning to get yourself going after a heavy drinking session?

    Never   less than monthly   monthly   weekly   daily or almost daily

7. How often during the last year have you had a feeling of guilt or remorse after drinking?

    Never   less than monthly   monthly   weekly   daily or almost daily

8. How often during the last year have you been unable to remember what happened the night before because you had been drinking?

    Never   less than monthly   monthly   weekly   daily or almost daily

9. Have you or someone else been injured as a result of your drinking?

    No   yes, but not in the last year   yes, during the last year

10. Has a relative or friend or a doctor or other health worker been concerned about your drinking or suggested you cut down?

    No   yes, but not in the last year   yes, during the last year

Scoring the AUDIT

Scores for each question range from 0 to 4, with the first response for each question (e.g. never) scoring 0, the second (e.g. less than monthly) scoring 1, the third (e.g. monthly) scoring 2, the fourth (e.g. weekly) scoring 3, and the last response (e.g. daily or almost daily) scoring 4. For questions 9 and 10, which only have 3 responses, the scoring is 0, 2 and 4 (from left to right).

A score of 8 or more is associated with harmful or hazardous drinking, a score of 13 or more in women, and 15 or more in men, is likely to indicate alcohol dependence.

* * * * *

Somewhat predictably, Colin's score was 29. The staff nurse reflected this back to him, and he appeared surprised which reinforces his being in the pre-contemplation stage of change. Colin then admitted to the nurse that he knew his drinking was bad, but "not that bad". Even if he chose not to act on his situation there and then, the nurse had achieved one of her aims, that of raising his awareness of his problem situation.

The resource pack that the staff nurse was referring to in this example was simple, and contained some basic information. One recommendation would be that each ward area prepares some basic leaflets and tools that can be handed out to patients and their relatives either on admission, or certainly prior to discharge. In this instance, it contained:

1. *A resource directory.* This is a short leaflet giving names, addresses and contact telephone numbers of local agencies that provide help and support for people with alcohol problems. It is helpful if each entry has a brief description of the type of service it offers to enable patients to make more informed choices of the agencies they would prefer to contact. For instance, an entry for Alcoholics Anonymous could give a contact telephone number with a short paragraph saying that they offer support to people who need help to stop drinking, and that they operate on an anonymous basis. An entry for the local Alcohol Problems clinic could have a similar entry, but give opening hours and the name of a contact person at the unit.

2. *Information for carers.* This leaflet contained information about support available for friends and families of people who have a drinking problem, and also some useful advice about the process of detoxification to enable them to offer practical support to the patient if he/she is undergoing this process.

3. *Dietary advice leaflet.* This contained information about the value of eating a well balanced diet including vitamins for protection against central nervous system damage.

4. *Alcohol and the body.* This was a basic information leaflet that highlighted the harmful effects of alcohol on different parts of the body.

Other leaflets could be added as appropriate to the patient's stage of change, such as a drinking diary, a decision chart, a time management chart, a mood chart, and these are discussed in subsequent chapters of this book.

The next case study is quite different, and takes place in an orthopaedic unit.

* * * * *

Case Study 2

James is 52 years old and has been admitted to the orthopaedic ward following an accident at work. He is married for the second time, and although his older two children have both left home and have families of their own, he has a 7-year-old son to his second wife.

James' primary nurse was concerned about him, as the day following his admission he seemed edgy and was keen to discharge himself, even though his leg needed surgery to apply external fixation to a difficult fracture. He was watching the door constantly, and had phoned home every half-an-hour to talk to his son. Eventually the nurse was able to persuade James to talk about what was worrying him, and he said that he feared for the safety of his son because his wife was drinking heavily and he didn't think that she could care for him. He had never told anybody before what was happening at home and was tearful, expressing feelings of shame, fear, guilt, and low self-esteem. He seemed to think it was his fault his wife drank because she needed him at home, but he needed to work to support the family.

This case study approaches pre-contemplative drinking from the perspective of the patient being the carer of a problem drinker and not the actual drinker. Velleman (2000: 65) argues that service providers largely ignore families who are affected by the drinking of one or more of their members. In this case, James is in a position where he is receiving help for an orthopaedic problem but, until the nursing staff became aware of his home situation, it is unlikely they would have been in a position to address this problem, as the focus of their care plan had understandably been the fracture and its associated care. The nature of humanistic nursing is such that the nurse is able to explore other issues with her patients as part of the dynamics of the therapeutic relationship, during which dialogue occurs that is objective and influences both parties. That influence in James' nursing situation was such that he felt able to disclose his worries.

There is ample evidence to suggest that living with problematic drinking in the household causes major difficulties. For instance, it is estimated that 80% of family violence cases and some 20–30% of child abuse cases involve alcohol (Velleman, 1992: 133). Hazardous drinking is associated with divorce and separation, and with recent serious problems with a relative or close friend (Coulthard *et al*, 2002). Al-Anon is a sister fellowship to Alcoholics Anonymous, and runs meetings specifically for the friends and families who have loved ones that problematically drink. Within their Twelve Step literature, they propose that the individual who is affected by another's drinking is powerless over that person's drinking and that his/her own life has become unmanageable as a result (Al-Anon UK, 1995).

The children of problem drinkers face their own unique difficulties and there is ample evidence to suggest that children and adolescents are particularly prone to showing strain, either in ill-health or poor school attendance (West and Prinz, 1987). This is demonstrated by the following two tables, obtained during a study carried out by Orford and Velleman (1990), which investigated young adults' recollections of growing up in a family with problem drinking parents. The study looked at 168 young adults and compared their experience with a control group of 81.

Table 2.1: Negative childhood experiences: Responses

	Offspring (%) (n = 168)	Comparisons (%) (n = 81)
Arrangements going wrong	50.3	25.0
Lack of social life for the family	67.9	38.8
Moving house a lot	27.3	18.8
Being on own a lot	47.3	25.0
Forced to participate in parents' rows	44.8	8.8
Being pulled between parents	51.5	20.0
Worry re: parents losing job	22.4	3.8
Fear of having to do without	22.4	6.3
Keeping secrets from one parent to protect another	33.9	10.0
Putting parent to bed	28.5	1.3
Having to take care of parent	27.3	7.5
Having to 'act older'	61.8	21.3

(Orford and Velleman, 1990)

Table 2.2: Family violence reported by offspring of parents with drinking problems and controls

	Children of problem drinkers (%) (n = 168)	Comparisons (%) (n = 81)
Parent-to-parent violence		
Serious and regular violence, over a prolonged period	12	1
Any serious and regular violence	12.5	1
Any serious and prolonged violence	21	1
Any regular and prolonged violence	26	4
Any serious violence	29	7
Any regular violence	27	5
Any prolonged violence	48	6
Any violence	66	21
Parent-to-child violence		
Serious and regular violence, over a prolonged period	9	4
Any serious and regular violence	11	5
Any serious and prolonged violence	14	6
Any regular and prolonged violence	18	5
Any serious violence	20	10
Any regular violence	21	6

	Children of problem drinkers (%)	Comparisons (%)
	(n = 168)	(n = 81)
Parent-to-child violence (contd)		
Any prolonged violence	30	15
Any violence (excluding controlled corporal punishment)	41	19
Any violence (including controlled corporal punishment)	59	77

The staff nurse looking after James was aware of the issues surrounding young people living in heavy drinking situations, but was keen not to over-generalise from the results of such studies, preferring instead to assess James' situation on an individual basis. This demonstrates an awareness of the need for critical review of the literature. The following is a critical incident recording that she made, the first section of which she recorded in James' notes, then used as a basis for reflecting on her actions during supervision. As can be seen, he was nursed using Peplau's model and was in the identification phase of the nurse-patient relationship:

James B: 02/02/00

Subjective/objective observations (identification phase).
1. James was distracted and unsettled. He had been given Cyclimorph® for pain with good effect, and was nil by mouth because he was going to theatres in the afternoon, but remained unsettled;

2. Four hourly observations showed him to have a borderline pyrexia and slight tachycardia: this was to be expected given his trauma, and required no immediate intervention other than to ensure James was comfortable and understood what was happening;

3. Intravenous saline was being administered through a peripheral line; observations of the site showed no redness or blockage.

I spoke to James and pointed out that he appeared worried about something. He discussed with me his home situation, and expressed concern about the safety of his young son. I asked how his son had been the last time he phoned, and James said that he was crying because 'Mummy had shouted at him, then she had fallen asleep in front of the television'. I asked James if he wanted us to help in any way, and expressed concern for his son's safety. James said that he wanted to go home and look after him. I felt that James was holding back a lot of fears and worries, so I quietly touched his hand and sat in silence with him for a few moments. James cried, and eventually disclosed that the situation at home had been getting out of hand for years because his wife was drinking gin and wine every day causing utter chaos. He did not know where to turn, and had not asked anybody for help before. I offered to put him in touch with Al-Anon family groups, but James refused saying that he felt too ashamed. I asked if there was anybody else in the family who could look after his son while he was in hospital, as I felt there was a safety issue and that the young boy could not stay at home in the current circumstances. James eventually agreed for me to contact his oldest daughter, the boy's half sister, who came up to the hospital with him in the evening to visit dad, having agreed to have him stay until James was well enough to go home.

James agreed to a family referral to the social work team for ongoing support.

* * * * *

Personal learning goals/issues:

1.   *I would like to review family members' support available locally*

2.   *I intend to add some more appropriate information to the ward resource pack, as the leaflets for families were not up to date and had been badly photocopied*

The staff nurse was able to use this recording as a reflective practice tool in her next supervision session. As a result of wanting to review the supports available, she discovered a significant amount of local help that had not been available at the time the ward pack was produced. This highlights the necessity for updating information periodically. Wiles *et al* (1996) suggested that there is a need for service providers to offer individualised information for patients and their carers. The staff nurse, as a result of the reflection that she carried out on her practice, has recognised that the leaflets in the ward file are now out of date and beginning to show their age. This would be an ideal opportunity for a template to be added to the ward computer so that a print-out could be produced, which could be individualised and given out new to each patient.

Hagenhoff *et al* (1994) found that nurses rated the need for information as less important than patients did, and also suggested that nurses select different information as being a priority to that suggested by their patients. If good, up-to-date, user-friendly information is available in clinical settings, it can help to reduce one barrier to help-seeking on the part of individuals. The provision of patient information rests within the domain of patient education, an important role for the nurse within the nurse-patient relationship. Morgan (1994) found that nurses tend to initiate educational processes that empower individuals, which must be seen as one of the goals of humanistic nursing, namely to develop human potential (Meleis, 1997: 190).

The fact that James' wife has not sought to address her problem or seek help for it is not in itself surprising. Thom (1984) found that women are less likely to seek help than men for their alcohol problem, and there are several barriers to such action. For instance, there are few services available that offer crèche facilities, appointment times tend to be rigid, and few services offer gender-specific support. Thom and Green (1996: 204) suggest that there are three broad areas to be addressed in encouraging women to come forward: problem recognition, perceived cost of taking action, and perceived acceptability of available services. If we relate these areas to James' situation with his wife, and place it in the context of James' receiving help from the staff nurse within the nurse-patient relationship, there are several strategies that may be adopted to help his situation and hopefully improve things for his wife.

- *Recognising the problem.* The staff nurse has helped James to move on by her supportive intervention. He has now been enabled to participate in his recovery from the fracture as a more active partner because he does not have to worry in the immediate situation about the care of his son while he is in hospital. Although it could be argued that the wife is not her patient, the nurse has a moral obligation to care (Fealy, 1995: 1138) and, as such, her actions as delivered from within a humanistic framework constitute caring directly for James, and indirectly for his son and wife. His wife is no longer going to be in the position of acting in denial about her problem with the partners in her husband's care (the GP, the ward team, the social worker), because knowledge of it has entered the public domain— the referral to the social work department. She has choices; she may chose not to attend the referral meeting, but her dissonance will be raised (see *Page 10*) and there will be some discomfort until she makes a decision. James has the support of the nurse and other agencies, should he accept. His son has the support of James and his elder sibling. The wife has the offer of support from the social work team and, should she choose it, other agencies

- *Perceived cost of taking action.* This is difficult to quantify in this example because we do not have the benefit of James' wife's thoughts and feelings, nor those of the rest of the family. However, the literature shows us that barriers to help-seeking include: increased stigma with women drinkers, family costs ('Will my son be taken away?'), fear, shame, and a belief that the problem is not serious enough for treatment (Thom, 1986). The staff nurse will be able to work with James through the medium of the nurse-patient relationship to offer information of help available, and to offer reassurance. This will empower James in his own discussions with his wife, and alleviate some of his worries. The staff nurse could also offer his wife some time when she visits to help alleviate any fears

- *Perceived availability of services available.* The staff nurse herself was taken aback at how much help was available compared to when the ward resource file was last updated. This is likely to be the same reaction for James and his wife, because unless they have had experience of help seeking, they are unlikely to be aware of just what support **is** available. It is important to set up a meeting with the social work team before James is discharged to ensure continuity of care. Should he change his mind about accepting help from Al-Anon or some other agency, it is again likely that a meeting could be arranged before he leaves the ward so that he has the chance to meet people and address any misconceptions prior to leaving.

Summary

Within this chapter, the need for clear information has been identified as being crucial to the patient's ability to move on from the pre-contemplation stage of change. Also important is addressing the needs of carers, because at this stage there is likely to be the most chaos within the household. The use of humanistic nursing principles has been shown to have a valid place in settings where such chaos abounds. The next chapter remains within this stage, but focuses on different settings.

References

Al-Anon UK (1995) *How Al-Anon Works*. Al-AnonUK, London

Coulthard M, Farell M, Singleton N, Meltzer H (2002) *Tobacco, Alcohol and other Substance Misuse and Mental Health*. The Stationery Office, London: Available at: www.statistics.gov.uk

Fealy GM (1995) Professional caring: the moral dimension. *J Adv Nurs* **22**(6): 1135–40

Hagenhoff B, Feutz C, Conn V, Sagehorn K, Moranville-Hunziker M (1994) Patient education needs as reported by congestive cardiac failure patients and their nurses. *J Adv Nurs* **19**(4): 685–90

Meleis A (1997) *Theoretical Nursing: Development and Progress*. Lippincott, Philadelphia

Moyers T (2000) New perspectives on motivation and change. In: Cooper D, ed. *Alcohol Use*. Radcliffe Medical Press, Abingdon

Morgan A (1994) Client education experiences in professional nursing practice—a phenomenological perspective. *J Adv Nurs* **19**(4): 792–801

Murray A (1992) Minimal intervention with problem drinkers. In: Plant M, Ritson B, Robertson R, eds. *Alcohol and Drugs: The Scottish Experience*. Edinburgh University Press, Edinburgh

Saunders JB, Aasland OG, Babor TF, de le Fuente JR, Grant M (1993) Development of the alcohol use disorders identification test (AUDIT): WHO collaborative project on early detection of persons with harmful alcohol consumption: II. *Addiction* **88**: 791–803

Smith B (1998). The problem drinker's lived experience of suffering: an exploration using hermeneutic phenomenology. *J Adv Nurs* **27**: 213–22

Thom B (1986) Sex differences in help-seeking for alcohol problems—1: The barriers to help-seeking. *Br J Addiction* **87**: 613–14

Thom B (1984) A process approach to women's use of alcohol services. *Br J Addiction* **79**: 377–82

Thom B, Green A (1996) Services for women: the way forward. In: Harrison L, ed. *Alcohol Problems in the Community*. Routledge, London

Tober G (1991) Helping the pre-contemplator. In: Davidson R, Rollnick S, MacEwan I, eds. *Counselling Problem Drinkers*. Routledge, London

Velleman R (2000) The importance of the family. In: Cooper D, ed. *Alcohol Use*. Radcliffe Medical Press, Abingdon

Velleman R (1992) *Counselling for Alcohol Problems*. Sage, London

West M, Prinz R (1987) Parental alcoholism and childhood psychopathology. *Psycholog Bull* **102**: 204–18

Wiles R, Pain H, Buckland S, McLellan L (1996) Providing appropriate information to patients and carers following a stroke. *J Adv Nurs* **28**(4): 794–801

3
Working with pre-contemplators 2: Primary health and outpatient settings

This chapter will again use a case study approach aimed at the practicalities of working with people who are reluctant attendees. They may only be participating in care because their wives/family/employer have said they need to, and not out of any serious commitment to change. It will discuss potential nursing care initiatives aimed at reducing harm in those who chose to continue drinking.

At the end of this chapter the reader will:

- Have a fuller understanding of the needs of pre-contemplators
- Understand one potential use of drinking diaries.

There is no doubt that the pre-contemplation stage of change can be a challenge for nurses offering support. The previous chapter demonstrated two individual situations involving people who were either unready to accept their own drinking problems, or who were affected by another person and their unaddressed drinking problem. Often, the reluctant attendee has come forward because of reasons, such as their spouse threatening to leave, or their employer expressing concern. In other words, the desire to change their drinking behaviour does not appear at the top of their agenda. The nature of this stage is that patients concentrate on issues and problems other than their drinking (Velleman, 1992). Thom (1987) found that there is a significant gap between the onset of problematic alcohol use and the time that individuals seek help for their behaviour, which in itself usually leads to an escalation of the problems.

When interventions are gauged at an appropriate level, appropriate support at this period of time in their drinking career also offers patients the chance to take the most significant step towards changing their behaviour and lifestyle. Detoxification with pre-contemplators is usually only carried out in urgent situations when deemed a medical priority, or from absolute necessity, such as when patients are a captive audience when they have been admitted to hospital for another reason, or even when they are in prison. However, this does not preclude other forms of support and help aimed at maintaining contact with patients, and at reducing the harm that their drinking is having on their health and well-being, including that of those around them.

* * * * *

The following case study discusses some of the issues that arose while caring for a gentleman within the community.

Case Study 3

Ronald is a 54-year-old man who lives with his elderly, disabled father (who has had a stroke) and their dog. He has been referred to the CPN by his GP who told the nurse that Ronald's liver enzymes were significantly impaired, that he was developing peripheral neuropathy and ataxia, and that he showed no inclination to change his behaviour but 'something has to be done'. At the first interview, Ronald was perplexed at needing to be there saying he'd always been a drinker and so had his father before he became ill, and his grandfather, and that the doctor had no right sending him in the first place; he also said that there wasn't really a problem. The nurse adopted an informal approach to their first session, taking no notes, and explained that he did not have to stay, but that she would like to spend some more time getting to know him to see if there was anything else he needed help with. At the end of this first session, it became clear that he needed more support looking after his father who was very demanding and watchful of him. He was able to recognise that some of his drinking was indeed an escape, and that it also interfered with his ability to walk the dog as often as he would like, but that he had no intention of stopping. He also agreed that, as he could not tell how much he was honestly drinking, he would fill in a drinking diary 'just out of curiosity'.

As can be seen from the above case study, Ronald is in the pre-contemplation stage of change. This is evidenced by his stated intention of not changing and his lack of acknowledgement that there was any real problem with his drinking.

* * * * *

The following is a short transcript from part of a supervision session between the CPN and her supervisor:

Supervisor = S

S: Why do you think he attended if he was so certain that he didn't have a problem?

CPN: *I think he felt coerced, to be honest. His GP had put a lot of pressure on him, and a lot of emphasis on the blood results.*

S: Did you talk about them with him?

CPN: *No. I let him tell me about them himself when he arrived, but I then decided not to bring the subject up again unless he did. To be honest, I felt that the GP could deal with that side of things, and it was more important that he felt he could open up and start talking to me. I kept thinking that if this referral was going to work, then I needed to demonstrate that I was willing to work with him even if he didn't feel ready to accept he had a problem. I was genuinely concerned in his situation, because he was drinking an indefinable amount of alcohol, he was clearly exhausted with looking after his Dad, and I felt that there was more we could offer him as a carer.*

S: Is that your job, do you think?

CPN: *Not directly, no. But as resource person I felt able to do a carer assessment and put him in touch with Crossroads[1], because that way one of the problems that he had would hopefully be taken care of for some of the time, giving him one less reason to drink....*

* * * * *

The CPN used this first referral session to try and develop a working relationship with Ronald as it was the orientation phase of the nurse-patient relationship, and she was aware that her style of care delivery is likely to influence whether or not he engages in care and attends again. Simpson (1991) talks of the relationship that develops between the nurse and the patient as being vital to the process of nursing, and argues that this is a dynamic skill, involving confidence on the part of the nurse. There is potential for conflict in this situation, as the nurse's background, knowledge and skills could lead her to believe that Ronald should change his drinking behaviour for health reasons, but Ronald's experience has led him to believe that there are other priorities in his life. Hester and Miller (1989) suggest that professionals who deal with problem drinkers in an empathic way, with humour and optimism, are more likely to generate success than those who use a confrontational approach. The CPN was warm and empathic with Ronald, at the same time maintaining one of the propositions of Paterson and Zderad at the core of the care planning, namely that 'Nursing's goal of more well-being is enhanced by both nurse and patient as they experience the process of making responsible choices' (Paterson and Zderad, 1976). This enabled her to encourage Ronald to reflect on his drinking behaviour, and the effect it was having on him, so that he would be able to begin the process of making change decisions at some stage in the future.

When the CPN completed a carer assessment and gave Ronald leaflets about Crossroads, she was effectively working at a level of change that sits besides the substance level. Prochaska and DiClemente describe their model as transtheoretical (Davidson, 1991). In other words, it is an eclectic approach to care that embraces differing therapeutic approaches to the explanation of, and influences on, addictive behaviours. In this instance, she was looking at the family unit as a source of problem behaviour for Ronald. The assumption would be, therefore, that helping him to resolve some of his stress related to the care of his father would remove some of his motivation to drink. This is controversial, as some schools of thought dictate that, for people to face up to their difficulties, they need to reach 'rock bottom', i.e. increased suffering will lead to behaviour change. This is particularly the case among some of the self-help groups, such as Alcoholics Anonymous. However, Tober (1991) argues that increased suffering can lead to accelerated drinking. Therefore, it seems reasonable for the CPN to help Ronald to remove some of the stressors in his life in an attempt to help him move on from his current thoughts about his drinking.

There is evidence to suggest that nutritional imbalance causes Wernicke's encephalopathy and eventually Korsakoff's psychosis in some heavy drinkers (Harper *et al*, 1986). During their discussion, Ronald disclosed that he rarely ate fruit or vegetables and, although he cooked for his father, he rarely ate any of the food himself as he lost his appetite when he cooked. The CPN knew that he needed to increase his thiamine intake to guard against the development of such disorders, and knew that his options were for dietary rigour or medicinal supplementation. The recently published SIGN Guidelines (Scottish

1   Crossroads for Carers—a national support organisation giving practical advice and support for carers.

Intercollegiate Guidelines Network, 2003) suggest that patients who have a chronic alcohol problem and whose diet may be deficient should be given oral thiamine indefinitely. In helping Ronald to decide how to redress any imbalance, the CPN is acting in the capacity of resource person by providing information about the need for thiamine in the diet. Moreover, Sanchez-Craig (1987) found that staff who are competent in the delivery of interventions, and knowledgeable about alcohol and its effects, are more likely to maintain contact with their clients. This is compatible with Peplau's notion that nursing is both educational and therapeutic (Peplau, 1988).

Date: <u>00/00</u>

Stage of change: Pre-Contemplation

Phase of the nurse-patient relationship: Orientation

Level of intervention: Substance

Partners in Ronald's care: Ronald, *CPN, GP? Crossroads*

Objective: 1) To help Ronald minimise the harm in his current drinking

2) To provide Ronald with some support and respite at home in his caring role

CARE PLAN

1)   Ronald will complete a drinking diary over the next week

2)   Ronald has agreed to eat a balanced diet during the week ahead

3)   Ronald has agreed to try not to drink alcohol before lunchtime

4)   The CPN has agreed to ask the GP for a thiamine prescription for Ronald

5)   The CPN has agreed to place a formal referral to Crossroads for Carers

Review date:

Signature:

Figure 3.1: Care plan, Pre-Contemplation

In terms of his actual drinking pattern, as already stated, Ronald was unwilling to accept that there was any major problem with his consumption. He had agreed, however, to fill in a diary to monitor both pattern and intake so that the information gathered could be used as a discussion point in their next meeting. The CPN was aware that if the initial meeting had not gone well, if they had not been able to develop some rapport between them, then Ronald was unlikely to fill it in. At his most chaotic drinking times, he would have neither the motivation nor the concentration to complete anything complicated, and she therefore chose a simple drinking diary in preference to something more detailed, which would really only be suitable for the person in determination/action who is getting ready to change and is planning how to do it. Mason (1989) argues that most people when asked how much they drink are unable to recall exact amounts because they are not counting at the time. As we saw in the introduction, units are difficult to assess because of the way alcohol is served in bars (no strength on the pumps in many establishments). There are many examples in the literature of the type of diary one can use, and the one provided here (*Figure 3.2*) is one such example. She also asked Ronald to try and delay the start of his daily drinking until his lunchtime meal, as she felt this would have the effect of reinforcing the need to eat, and would reduce the amount he drank, even if only by a few units.

The care plan that they eventually compiled together demonstrates an acknowledgement that there are several issues Ronald needs to address in order to reduce the harm that he is currently facing because of the choices he has made about his drinking to date. It sets out clearly the actions that both the CPN and Ronald are expected to complete, therefore reinforcing the collaborative approach to care that the CPN has adopted within a humanistic perspective.

When Ronald returned, he had managed to follow some of the advice given, but felt he hadn't really needed to reduce the amount because he still did not think his consumption was excessive. However, the diary was filled in with enough details for the CPN to begin exploring some of Ronald's conceptions about drinking levels, and for a very tentative move towards some motivational work as will be described in later chapters. Ronald did not know how many units he had been drinking, for instance, giving the CPN the opportunity for some educational work with him. On the days that he had not filled in the diary he had said it was a bad day—this could be at odds with the history he gave at the first session when he did not think he had a problem if it turned out that the bad day was related to drink. The diary was not filled in exactly how it was intended to be, as is nearly always the case. Whereas we cannot expect all of our patients to fill these forms in perfectly, it may well be that the forms have to be adapted the second time round to fit in with the patient's frame of reference, and the nurse has to re-evaluate her teaching methods to check out understanding and clarity. The simpler the better is often the most appropriate guideline. Mumford (1997) argues that any information leaflets produced locally for patients should be assessed for readability, as health care workers cannot assume that all patients have the same reading ability. There are other physical difficulties inherent in producing leaflets and charts such as this drinking diary; for example, with the text and typeface used; Ariel 14 is recommended where possible because the text is large enough and clear enough for most people to see. Shiny printing paper should be avoided because glare can affect visibility in the visually impaired, and it is recommended that lower case is used instead of capitalisation for the same reasons. If the computer used has a grammar check, then a high readability score is indicative of ease of reading; likewise a Flesch Kincaid score aiming for 8 would indicate that most people educated to the age of 14 would have no difficulty reading it.

The CPN accepted what Ronald had written with enthusiasm and gratitude, giving appropriate praise for the effort that he had put in to the exercise. The following (*Figure 3.2*) is the completed diary.

Day	What did I drink?	Where/When/ With Whom/ How much?	How many Units	Total (Units and Cost)
Monday				
Tuesday	Cider, whisky	1 bottle of cider in the house (2 litres) during the day, and ¾ bottle of whisky. By myself.	Don't know	About £10 I suppose
Wednesday	Same as yesterday			
Thursday	Whisky, some tins of strong lager	1 bottle of whisky, 4 tins lager at home		£15
Friday	Beer and Whisky	The Royal after lunch. A couple of pints then some whisky at home.		£15
Saturday	Beer, Whiskey carry out	The Royal in the afternoon — football was on— Sister took Dad for the day. Loads of pints. Had a half bottle for a carry out.		Spent £40
Sunday		Drank my carry out before 10 — had a hangover. Some more cans and another half bottle at night.		£9
Total for week:				

Figure 3.2: Drinking diary

At the end of the second session, Ronald was more willing to consider his drinking as problematic. The CPN, who wanted him to look at some of his stated reasons for drinking, and at some of his beliefs about his drinking pattern, asked him to answer a quiz from a pre-printed booklet, which he was asked to bring with him to his next appointment. In doing this, the CPN was acting in the role of educator, but using a facilitative style—encouraging Ronald to develop problem-solving skills of his own. This is similar to the quiz used.

Please note: 'having a dram' is Ronald's way of saying having a drinking session; the CPN has used the phrase to make the form more appealing to Ronald:

Ronald—please think about the following statements, and then decide whether they apply to you.	Please circle your answer	
Having a dram makes me feel relaxed	Yes	No
I like the taste of my drinks	Yes	No
Having a dram makes me feel less tired	Yes	No
I sleep better after having a dram	Yes	No
My friends would not want to know me if I didn't have a dram	Yes	No
I would not enjoy the football if I didn't have a dram	Yes	No
If I didn't have the pub to go to I would have nowhere else	Yes	No
I can have a good laugh if I have had a dram	Yes	No
If I cut down my drinking there would be no point in anything	Yes	No
Everyone else drinks as much as me, they don't have a problem	Yes	No
Sometimes I want to change what I drink, sometimes I don't see any point	Yes	No
I would have more energy for the dog and other things if I didn't have a dram	Yes	No

Figure 3.3: Drinking Quiz

There are no right or wrong answers here; each question has been worded to provide a body of opinion which will guide the next session between the CPN and Ronald. The answers will help her to begin to measure his motivation to change, and to have a firm idea of some of his conceptions about drink and the effect it is having on his life. All of this will help prepare Ronald for moving into contemplation.

* * * * *

Case Study 4

Jimmy is a 52-year-old man who attends a drop in centre on a regular basis. He is known as a binge drinker locally, spending several weeks sober before drinking problematically for a few weeks at a time during which he often ends up in difficulties. One afternoon, an outreach worker from the local centre brought him to Accident and Emergency (A&E), saying that she found him collapsed behind the car park, and that, although she knew he was drunk, she thought he had other medical problems as his breathing appeared laboured. On examination, he was intoxicated, but appeared cyanosed and had a productive cough, and the duty doctor wondered if he had pneumonia. It was difficult to assess him because he was acting in a belligerent fashion. The doctor felt she could not assess him, nor treat him, until he sobered up a little more, but was keen that he stayed in the department and not be allowed to leave. She wanted to have full investigations taken of his physical condition, and wanted to admit him to the medical unit for detoxification and treatment. The staff nurse was able to secure a quiet area of the department for him to remain, but was worried that because they were so busy with other attendees he was not receiving the attention he deserved

Binge drinking in men is usually associated with drinking ten or more units of alcohol at a time, and in women seven (Paton, 2000: 28). So if an average bottle of wine contains 9 units of alcohol, any woman drinking a whole bottle in one session has technically had a binge. Likewise, if an average bottle of whisky contains 30 units of alcohol, then drinking a third of a bottle in one session is technically considered a binge. Clearly, there are going to be occasions where most social drinkers will drink what constitutes a binge using these indicators, i.e. at a wedding or on other such festive events, and they will come to no ill harm other than an occasional hangover, hence this definition alone is inadequate.

Binge drinking in this context is associated with heavy drinking that leads to a rapid onset of problems, followed by a period of calm usually brought about by enforced abstinence—when individuals can no longer physically drink alcohol for a few days because they feel so ill. In Jimmy's case, he has drunk enough alcohol to induce intoxication as evidenced by his behaviour in the department, and at the same time mask an underlying medical condition that may or may not have been precipitated by his lifestyle or drinking choices.

It is estimated that one in ten of all A&E admissions are alcohol-related (Scottish Executive, 2002), posing significant problems for the staff on duty. Increasing levels of violence towards the nurses in particular are a great worry, with many hospitals recruiting security staff to patrol areas. This may give the staff some sense of protection and security, but it can be distressing for other users who attend the department, but who do not want to feel as if they are in a custodial setting. Likewise, drunken belligerent behaviour in the waiting room is unacceptable for anyone attending, so there needs to be a creative solution. It is expected that if the person attending is merely intoxicated, they would be asked to leave and, if necessary, removed by force from the department as a safety measure. If the attendee has a genuine reason for his/her presence, then risk assessment must take priority as the initial action (unless the attendee is unconscious or a medical emergency).

Risk assessment in this example dictated that the staff were made aware of the condition of the patient, that he was nursed in a safe area where there were no sharp instruments or other objects that he could endanger himself or others with, and that the environment was calm with no excess stimulation. The doctor requested that he be monitored until he was less intoxicated, and then he could be examined properly including chest X-rays and blood tests; she was also keen to start a detoxification using the unit's symptom severity assessment chart (see *Chapter 6*) as soon as was appropriate. The staff nurse who was allocated as his named nurse for the duration of Jimmy's stay chose to use a nursing diagnosis tool for his alcohol problem care plan, as he would only need to be in the department for a few hours and she felt that when he was admitted to the ward, and by using this tool, they would be able to continue with his care and assessment when he was less intoxicated. This in itself would ensure continuity of care.

Nursing diagnosis has been described as :

'A clinical judgement about individual, family or community responses to actual or potential problems/life processes. Nursing diagnoses provide the basis for selection of nursing interventions to achieve outcomes for which the nurse is accountable'.

(NANDA, 1990, cited in Carpentino, 1995)

The system of developing nursing diagnoses for use as care planning tools evolved in the 1970s and 80s; they are the product of several conferences attended by many nurses who used their time together to reflect on clinical practice, and to develop a common methodology for assessing, planning, delivering and evaluating care. They are written using a PES format, where P = problem statement, E = aetiology, and S = signs and symptoms. Their reductionist approach, although at odds with holism in nursing, does offer clear measurable steps to providing evidence-based care, and the one advantage in an acute, time-limited setting is the time saved in drawing out a new care plan for each occasion.

As a nursing approach, nursing diagnosis is able to sit comfortably with any philosophy of care, as it provides the mechanics of care to be delivered throughout the chosen paradigm. When used within a humanist paradigm, for instance, the nurse's ability to be with the patient in a meaningful interaction is not affected adversely by having the care plan pre-printed and referenced. In other words, nursing diagnoses are not incongruous with a humanist model of care; what needs to happen for them to have greater utility is that their wording be altered to reflect the underlying paradigm, thus providing a shift from their positivist stance. *Figure 3.3* is one example of the type of plan applicable here:

NURSING DIAGNOSIS: *Risk of injury related to alcohol withdrawal*

EXPECTED PATIENT OUTCOME:

■ The patient will experience a decrease in symptoms indicative of alcohol withdrawal with no physical harm to self.

NURSING INTERVENTIONS WITH RATIONALE:

1. Provide a safe and monitored environment that has minimal external stimulation to decrease possibility of agitation, anxiety and belligerence caused by central nervous system (CNS) stimulation during withdrawal (Morofka, 1993)
2. Initiate monitoring of initial symptoms using an approved severity of withdrawal chart recognising that symptoms can begin within 6–8 hours after the client's last drink.
3. To the extent possible, obtain information from the family, friends, records and health care providers about the client's history as factors, such as severity of previous withdrawal, are a predictor of future withdrawals.
4. Arrange for a mental state examination to be carried out soon, as continued drinking is a risk factor for suicide in alcoholics.
5. Monitor physical status regularly, as alcohol withdrawal increases the risk for hypertension, tachycardia and pyrexia.
6. Ensure adequate food and oral fluid intake because of risk of dehydration, and to encourage increased vitamin and nutrient intake.
7. Monitor the effect of prescribed medication using an approved chart, and monitor compliance. Do not under-medicate because early intervention reduces the severity of the withdrawal (McFarland *et al*, 1997); inadequate treatment may increase potential for future relapse during treatment, and also increases the chance of complications such as withdrawal fits.
8. Collaborate with other health care professionals in the administration of other medication such as parenteral thiamine which prevents the development of Wernicke-Korsakoff syndrome.
9. Ensure that the client has a quiet night-time environment to promote relaxation and sleep; using a nightlight minimises distortion of environmental stimuli.

Date of initial assessment:

Dates for review of plan:

All references to be found in: McFarland G, Wasli E, Gerety E (1997) *Nursing Diagnosis and Process in Psychiatric Mental Health Nursing*. Lippincott, Philadelphia

Figure 3.3 Nursing Diagnosis Care Plan: acute area detoxification

The following is a transcript of part of a reflective practice group session facilitated by a nurse tutor who is also responsible for supervising students in the acute area:

* * * * *

Staff Nurse = SN; Facilitator = F; Peer = P

SN: *It's just so frustrating, I was trying really hard to keep an eye on him, but the lady with the gynae problems was distressed and I felt I had to spend more time with her so Jimmy was ignored.*

F: Ignored?

SN: *Well, maybe not ignored completely ... I was really unsure about how much of what was happening he was taking in. And he wouldn't keep his oxygen mask on when he was awake, I was terrified he would light up a ciggie and we'd end up having a fire.*

F: How did you manage to resolve this?

SN: *I pulled the nursing assistant from the fracture clinic to boost the numbers in the bay, and asked her to watch him. I don't think the charge nurse was best impressed with the doctor, and Jimmy by rights should have gone up to the ward sooner... the whole situation shows just the kind of pressure we are under at times.*

P: Was he in withdrawals? Had he had a fit before or any other complications?

SN: *When he arrived he was just intoxicated, but after a few hours we noticed he became more agitated. I know that the onset of withdrawals is likely to be between 6 and 24 hours after stopping, and it didn't seem as if he had been drinking for a few hours prior to coming in because he had been in a collapsed state in the car park. We had the doctor sign the SSA[2] chart and script so that we could medicate early to reduce the chance of any problems developing. We found out later when his previous records arrived that he did have withdrawal seizures, but he was fine in the department this time.*

* * * * *

This transcript is a useful reminder of the frustration that one feels when nursing patients who are intoxicated, and of the practical difficulties of managing this in A&E departments. However, it also serves to demonstrate the usefulness of reflective practice sessions, as several issues emerged. In the first instance, both the supervisor and the peer acting in a catalytic facilitative style highlight the supportive nature of supervised reflective practice. This technique relies upon reflective questions being asked that encourage the participants to look back on their practice and talk about issues in a way that helps them to move on. It mirrors the counselling process, when counsellors ask their clients to reflect on events in order to help them to make sense of their situation.

The staff nurse was able to say in the group what she did to overcome the practical difficulty—changing the work structure for a short period of time by re-allocating the nursing assistant. When one feels frustrated, or that one could have done more, then by recognising what one actually did in a given situation and how it worked will positively reinforce the strategy and improve confidence. If it had not worked out as well, then the discussion could have led into some group problem-solving to develop a strategy to try should the situation re-occur.

Another valuable aspect of reflection on practice that is demonstrated here is the function of drawing out the theory underpinning practice. The staff nurse was able to discuss the

---

2   SSA chart: symptom severity assessment chart; see *Chapter 6*.

onset of withdrawal symptoms, and the medical management of them using symptom severity assessment charts with appropriate prescribing. This serves as a reminder that theory is ingrained in our actions, and also serves as a peer education process for those members of the group that may not be as experienced in some areas of practice.

Summary

This chapter has served to illustrate some of the practicalities of working with pre-contemplative patients in two distinctly different settings. It has also illustrated peer reflection (as opposed to reflection with line managers or an individual facilitator). Whereas nursing diagnoses have been shown to have a role in some settings, such as the busy A&E department, there is scope for nurses who are considering using them in settings with patients with alcohol problems to critically investigate the values inherent within them (Lützén and Tishelman, 1996: 199) for them to have greater utility. This chapter has also demonstrated some of the techniques used to encourage patients who are pre-contemplative to move on in their view of their problematic drinking by the use of creative, individualised questionnaires. The next chapter will now progress into the contemplation stage of change.

References

Carpentino L (1995) *Nursing Diagnosis: Application to Clinical Practice*, 6th edn. Lippincott. Philadelphia

Davidson R, Rollnick S, MacEwan I (1991) *Counselling Problem Drinkers*. Routledge, London

Harper CG, Giles M, Finlay-Jones R (1986) Clinical signs in the Wernicke-Korsakoff Complex—A retrospective analysis of 131 cases diagnosed at autopsy. *J Neurol Neurosurg Psychiatry* **49**: 341–45

Hester R, Miller WR, eds (1989) *Handbook of Alcoholism Treatment Approaches: Effective Approaches*. Pergamon, Oxford

Lützén K, Tishelman C (1996) Nursing diagnosis: a critical analysis of underlying assumptions. *Int J Nurs Stud* **33**(2): 190–200

McFarland G, Wasli E, Gerety E (1997) *Nursing Diagnosis and Process in Psychiatric Mental Health Nursing*. Lippincott, Philadelphia

Mason 1989) *Managing Drink*. Aquarius, Birmingham

Morofka V (1993) Mental health. In: Thompson JM, McFarland GK, Hirsch JE, Tucker SM eds. *Mosby's Clinical Nursing* 3rd edn. Mosby Year Book, St Louis

Mumford M (1997) A descriptive study of the readability of patient information leaflets. *J Adv Nurs* **26**(5): 985–92

Paterson JG, Zderad LT (1976) *Humanistic Nursing*. John Wiley and Sons, New York

Paton A (2000) The body and its health. In: Cooper D, ed. *Alcohol Use*. Radcliff Medical Publishing, Abingdon

Peplau H (1988) *Interpersonal Relations in Nursing*. 2nd edn. Macmillan, Basingstoke

Sanchez-Craig M (1987) Short term treatment: conceptual and practical issues. Paper presented at *Fourth International Conference on the Treatment of Addictive Behaviours*, Norway. In: Tober G (1991)

Scottish Executive (2002) *A Plan for Action on Alcohol Problems*. Scottish Executive, Edinburgh: (available at: www.scotland.gov.uk/health/alcoholproblems)

Scottish Intercollegiate Guidelines Network (2003) *Management of Harmful Drinking and Alcohol Dependence in Primary Care: Guideline 74*; September 2003. SIGN, Edinburgh

Simpson H (1991) *Peplau's Model in Action*. Macmillan, Basingstoke

Thom B (1987) Sex differences in help-seeking for alcohol problems—2. Entry into treatment. *Br J Addiction* **81**: 777–88

Tober G (1991) Helping the pre-contemplator. In: Davidson R, Rollnick S, MacEwan I, eds. *Counselling Problem Drinkers*. Routledge, London

Velleman R (1992) *Counselling for Alcohol Problems*. Sage, London

4
Nursing the undecided

This chapter will focus almost entirely on motivational issues, and challenging ambivalence by raising cognitive dissonance in those patients who are undecided about changing their drinking behaviour; it uses case studies and reflective practice transcripts as a means of exploring problem-solving techniques. This chapter will illustrate that nurses in various settings have skills to offer such patients, even though the type of interventions used may have been seen as rooted in the domain of the specialist agencies.

At the end of this chapter, the reader will have a greater understanding of:

- The contemplation stage of change
- The use of decision charts and drinking diaries
- Brainstorming potential solutions with patients
- Health promotion
- The use of reflective journals

The contemplation stage of change is marked predominantly by signs of ambivalence within individuals. Crucially, these patients are beginning to acknowledge that there is a link between their current problem situation and their drinking behaviour, even if that acknowledgement is somewhat tentative. It is also important to stress that motivation here is considered unstable (Velleman, 1992) as, unlike the pre-contemplator who is evidently wanting to drink and has little or no motivation to change, the contemplator is changing his/her mind, almost by the hour.

When a patient presents for help demonstrating signs of ambivalence then, whatever the setting, each nurse has skills to offer that will help individuals to make some firm decisions about their drinking behaviour. The following two case studies, with reflective discussion, highlight some of the potential issues for consideration by practitioners and some possible nursing approaches.

* * * * *

Case Study 4

Ron, 49 years of age, lives with his wife Helen in a remote cottage. At first interview with his CPN, he discussed the problems that his wife was experiencing because of her Parkinson's disease and said that she became tired and weepy, and didn't like it when he went to the pub for a break. When the CPN explored his situation with him, he disclosed that he was drinking the equivalent of upwards of 350 units of alcohol a week, that he was not eating, and that they were in debt because of money he had spent on at least two bottles of vodka a day. He also noticed that he had some numbness and tingling in his feet, and that the doctor had told him he had signs of liver disease, although he didn't fully understood what the GP had said. The CPN asked him if he felt his problems were due to his drinking and he replied that, although he knew the drinking didn't help as it caused debt, he felt that his home situation was also a cause, and that if he was honest he still got some relief from his problems. The CPN then asked him to talk about the positive benefits he was experiencing with alcohol, before moving on to ask him to talk about the negative effects it was having. At the end of this first session, she summarised what they had talked about, then set a homework task by asking Ron to complete a decision matrix (see below), and Ron agreed that he would try and eat one meal a day until the next session. He also said that he would try and halve his consumption of alcohol using a drinking diary, because he recognised that the current level was not safe, but did not feel ready to stop. The CPN agreed to find out about support for the family from the Parkinson's nurse, and agreed to find out more about what the GP had said.

* * * * *

From the above case study, we can see that Ron is in the early stages of contemplation. This is evidenced by ambivalence, and a tentative acknowledgement that his alcohol consumption was contributing to his problems. At the end of the session, the CPN prepared the following care plan using Peplau's model as a means of care delivery within the framework of the model of change:

Date: 00/00

Stage of change: Contemplation

Phase of the nurse-patient relationship: Identification

Level of intervention: Substance

Partners in Ron's care: *Ron, CPN, GP, Wife, ?Parkinson's Nurse Specialist*

Objective: To help Ron resolve his ambivalence towards change decisions.

CARE PLAN:

1) Ron will complete a decision matrix, and bring it to the next session on *(date)*

2) Ron has agreed to eat one meal a day before the next session. This will be well balanced, as discussed and agreed with *(CPN)*

3) Ron will fill in a drinking diary to monitor his alcohol consumption, which he will bring to the next session

4) *(CPN)* will speak to Dr X, and find out Ron's blood results. This information will be given to Ron at the next session.

Review date:

Signature:

Figure 4.1: Care plan: Contemplation

Note that Ron and the CPN included the Parkinson's nurse on the list of partners; this is an acknowledgement that she will have an important role with the family unit. Here is an excerpt from a reflective practice session between the CPN and her supervisor:

＊ ＊ ＊ ＊ ＊

Community Psychiatric Nurse = N; Supervisor = S

N: *At first, I thought he was still in pre-contemplation .. you see, he really focussed on his wife's problems at first, you know, her Parkinson's disease, and the problems that caused them.*

S: What made you think otherwise?

N: *Well, he started talking about debt and stuff, and said that he had some tingling which I took to be a peripheral nerve problem caused by alcohol. So I asked him directly if he thought his drinking had contributed. He said yes—albeit reluctantly.*

S: What happened next?

N: *Well, we chatted for a bit, and I asked him to tell me some more about the positive effect his drinking was having on him. He really opened up then, and I felt he could have talked for hours on the subject. Anyway, at the end I summarised everything for him, and we negotiated some objectives. He agreed to eat a meal every day, which I was pleased about because he had been getting all of his calories from alcohol. I felt that he still needed time to look into the pros and cons of change, so I gave him a decision chart to fill in. He agreed that the amount he was drinking was dangerous, and was going to reduce by half.*

S: Reduce by half? How was he going to do this?

N: *I gave him a drinking diary, and we talked through a plan that he felt would work for him. To be honest, I was really uncomfortable …*

S: Uncomfortable?

N: *Aye—I mean, the government tell men no more than 3 or 4 units a day, and one or two alcohol free days a week, and here I am helping someone plan to drink 30 a day! I justified this though by recognising it was less than he had been, and I felt that if I asked more of him he would back off, because he wasn't quite ready to make the commitment to change.*

* * * * *

At the beginning of this session, the CPN thought that Ron was in the pre-contemplation stage of change as evidenced by his initial discussion of the current problems, which he appeared to see as rooted within his wife's experience. This is typical of the pre-contemplator's experience, where the alcohol consumption is secondary to any other problem they may have, and is not necessarily seen as causative. However, using Peplau's model of nursing as her means of care delivery, it was possible for the CPN to encourage Ron to begin to explore his situation from his own perspective, hence identifying some ambivalence regarding his alcohol consumption and a tentative acceptance that perhaps his drinking was a contributing factor. Peplau describes nursing as 'a significant, therapeutic, interpersonal process' (Peplau, 1988) and this session took place during the orientation phase of that process. During this time, the CPN is seen as helping the patient to become orientated to his or her new situation—in Ron's case, acknowledging and understanding how his drinking is contributing to his current difficulties (Simpson, 1991).

If Peplau's model and the development of the nurse-patient relationship, as outlined in *Figure 1.1* (*Page 5*) is related directly to this case study, then Ron and his CPN have met as strangers with their own attitudes and   values about health. By exploring his current situation from Ron's own perspective, they are developing a mutual understanding of his problems and are able to work on common goals, even though each has their own roles within the process.

It is essential in this early stage that the nurse ensures she becomes aware of how much her patient understands of his condition and also ways in which she needs to be a knowledgeable practitioner for him. This informs the practice with relation to the homework tasks for both Ron and the nurse. In order for Ron to become more knowledgeable about his own condition, the CPN in this example has acted in two distinct ways: firstly, she is seeking clarification on Ron's behalf from the medical team. This will inform the next session, during which she can become an information source. Secondly, she is helping him to raise his own awareness of his problem by affording the opportunity for self-exploration by means of the decision chart. This is a key factor in motivational interviewing as described by Miller (1983), during which patients are encouraged to take self responsibility for their drinking behaviour. Specifically, using various therapeutic techniques, it is possible to help patients make a decision about changing their behaviour by raising their cognitive dissonance. During this process, the patient is encouraged to recognise the inconsistency between what he/she is doing, and his/her personal beliefs and attitudes. In this case, Ron is encouraged to reflect on his own statement that he knows he should stop drinking because it is causing debt. The drinking diary is a tool used in this instance to inform Ron's choice about his future drinking plans. Baldwin (1991) argues that it can be seen as a weak method of behaviour change, but Raistrick (1991) advocates that the appropriate use of such a method may well help self-monitoring of the drinking. Ron appeared to monitor his consumption by how much money he had spent on alcohol (the equivalent of two bottles of spirits a day). However, by focussing more closely on his consumption, an accurate picture may well be drawn that incorporates how much of his alcohol he may share with his fellow drinkers.

Figure 4.2 is the diary given to Ron which he brought back the following week. Note that it had been adapted to focus on the money he has spent rather than the focus being on the units. This is intentional, as Ron's stated measure is the money. Drinking diaries can be adjusted to meet individual requirements and as long as he has put the brand or strength of the drink, the CPN is still able to convert what he has written into units. Also note that, unlike the diary which is discussed in *Chapter 7*, it has no focus on rewards for achieving his preferred level of drinking. This again was intentional, as this was the first act of monitoring and not part of a controlled drinking programme. Its intention was as a self-assessment tool, and the nurse's intention was partly paradoxical in her approach. There was an element of demonstrating to Ron how difficult it was going to be for him to change from the level of drinking he was at. From the information that he gave to the CPN, she was able to determine that he was drinking at least 210 units of vodka, but this was an improvement because it represented only one bottle each day; however, she also determined that he was drinking more in the pub than he had realised. *Figure 4.3* is the decision matrix which the CPN asked him to complete. The information from both was then used in future sessions to provide a basis for change. One issue that emerged, for instance, was the role of Ron's pal Billy in his drinking. Ron did in fact agree to undergo detoxification quite soon after this session, with the intention of trying controlled drinking in the future.

Ron's Drinking Diary

Day	What did I plan to drink?	What did I actually drink?	Circumstances	Total cost
Monday	1 bottle blue label vodka	1 bottle + 3 or 4 pints of 80 Bob in pub	Billy's birthday, I forgot it was this week	A fortune!
Tuesday	1 bottle blue label vodka	¾ bottle + 3 or 4 pints		£22 ish
Wednesday	1 bottle blue label vodka	¼ bottle from yesterday + some of Billy's whisky	Had no money to buy any more.	Nothing.
Thursday	1 bottle blue label vodka	1 ½ bottles	payday	A fortune
Friday	1 bottle blue label vodka	1 ½ bottle	Finished off the yesterday's then bought some for today	£17
Saturday	1 bottle blue label vodka	1 bottle	At home. Football.	£17
Sunday	1 bottle blue label vodka	1 bottle and a dram or 2 at the pub	With Billy	£30 ish
Total for week:				About £120 in all

Figure 4.2: Drinking diary

Decision Balance Sheet			
If I decide to cut down my drinking to a safe level (2 or 3 pints a day of beer, or the equivalent in vodka)			
The benefits would be		The drawbacks would be	
Short term	Long term	Short term	Long term
I would have more money in my wallet	*I would be able to pay off the council tax debt and the credit card* *I would probably feel healthier* *Helen would stop nagging me as much*	*My hands would be shaky* *I would be grumpy and irritable* *I would have flashing lights before my eyes*	*Don't know. Can't really think of any.*
If I decide to carry on drinking at this level			
The benefits would be		The drawbacks would be	
Short term	Long term	Short term	Long term
I wouldn't have to think about all of this	*Oblivion*	*I would be absolutely skint* *The bailiffs will come* *I will be even more ill.*	*I will probably end up dead*

Figure 4.3: One form of decision matrix, as used by Ron

* * * * *

Case Study 5

Anne is a 45 year old housewife who has two children, a son who has left school and a daughter who is in her final year of study before university. Her husband is a local builder, and works long hours with an inconsistent income, so Anne feels great pressure to both keep the home in a manner to which they have all become accustomed, and to earn money to supplement the family income. She does this by working in a local hotel, which has in the past also been the focus of her drinking. She was admitted to a local hospital in status epilepticus following an alcohol withdrawal seizure, and had a cardiac arrest in the A&E department. Following detoxification from alcohol and cardiac rehabilitation, the staff nurse was preparing a discharge package of care for Anne.

It became clear that Anne had thought long and hard about how much her drinking had contributed to her current situation, and she told the staff nurse that she intended to make changes "but I have to admit, Nurse, I would still like to drink at parties!" The nurse decided to refer her to the local CPN on discharge, as she felt that Anne needed ongoing support, but she also felt that there was more that could be done from the ward. It was not the first admission for Anne, and the nurse recognised her own feelings of discomfort that nothing had really changed since her last admission. After consulting her community colleagues, she gathered some information leaflets on the nature of alcohol problems, and then spent an hour with Anne during which some of her difficulties and options for future employment were discussed.

As can be seen from the above example, Anne is in the contemplation stage of change. This is evidenced by marked signs of ambivalence ("but I would still like to drink at parties.."). At the end of their discussion, the staff nurse amended Anne's care plan to reflect the impending discharge. The following is a copy of the plan relating to her alcohol misuse (note: this does not include the cardiac rehabilitation care plan):

Date: 00/00

Stage of change: Contemplation

Phase of the nurse/patient relationship: Resolution

Level of intervention: Substance

Partners in Anne's care: *Anne, Ward team, CPN*

Objective: For Anne to leave the ward safely and be able to work

towards resolving her feelings of ambivalence towards her drinking.

CARE PLAN:

1) Anne will brainstorm a list of job alternatives to pursue in the future and write them down to discuss with the CPN.

2) (Nurse) will gather a discharge package of information on alcohol and general health issues.

3) (Nurse) will refer Anne to the local community psychiatric nurse (CPN) for some motivational interviewing and supportive counselling.

Review date:

Signed:

Figure 4.4: Care plan; contemplation

The staff nurse completed a critical incident recording in her reflective journal of the conversation she had with Anne. This is a simple statement for use as a reflective tool, in order to help nurses draw out the theory underpinning their practice. Atkins and Murphy (1993) describe reflection on action as a cognitive post mortem, during which nurses are able to look back at their actions and make explicit the knowledge, either in writing or in reflective discussion with a supervisor (or peer). The following is the recording which was used for self-reflection, as the staff nurse did not have supervision booked for that month. Note that the initial part of the recording is a subjective expression of the frustration that she feels as Anne's primary nurse.

Anne appears to listen to what we were advising, but in the next breath she talks about how she will be buying some liqueurs to see in the New Year with her husband and family. I feel that I should be able to say something or do something that will make her open her ears properly and hear what we have to say, but it seems it will never happen. I look at her family, visiting after work, and I worry that the next time she will arrest at home with nobody there to help her.

I have referred her to the CPN; I do not know if this will help, as Anne is very wilful and has a habit of doing her own thing no matter what is suggested. The CPN suggested that Anne do a brainstorm of potential jobs that she could try for—when I saw Anne doing it I was really taken aback; she has a lot of ambition and seemed almost embarrassed, crossing out things like teacher training, thinking that she wasn't good enough to even try. I spent some time with Anne, and told her that I felt she could turn her hand to whatever she wanted when she had the drinking sorted out. Anne was really happy with me saying this, I get the feeling that she doesn't have very much self-esteem. I know this goes hand in hand with chronic drinking, so maybe what is happening now for Anne is that she is starting to re-evaluate more than just her drinking.

I feel that two aspects of my role here are going to be important for Anne —health promoter, and empowerment. I intend to discuss both concepts with my supervisor, as I feel I need further training in the former, and would like to look at the latter in relation to the ward philosophy.

Figure 4.5: Reflective journal entry

The opening sentence of the staff nurse's reflective journal mirror's Anne's ambivalence. On the one hand she feels Anne is listening, on the other Anne talks about buying alcohol. Whereas this can be seen as a form of process comment, a simple statement of fact; as the nurse sees it, there is something much more subtle afoot. In humanistic nursing, there is an intellectual awareness, a meeting between the nurse and the patient, which Paterson and Zderad (1988) refer to as an inter-subjectivity. This is not dissimilar to the transference and counter-transference of a therapy relationship, in which the therapist experiences feelings from the patients and transfers them back in a way that both can work with. Reynolds and Scott (1999) talk of empathy as a crucial component of the helping relationship, and believe that its presence is crucial to a non-defensive relationship. In the situation between the staff nurse and Anne, we can see in that one opening sentence that the staff nurse has empathised with Anne— she is seeing and experiencing Anne's dilemma with Anne, then communicating that into her journal.

Menzies (1970) described how nurses avoid such depth of conversation by limiting the closeness with their patients as a protection against just this sort of anxiety. The use of reflective practice, clinical supervision and journals can, however, help convert this anxiety into a learning experience for the nurse and helps to maintain the principles of humanistic nursing.

By experiencing Anne's dilemma with her and reflecting on it, the staff nurse has been able to move on and recognise that a referral to the CPN was important to commence motivational interviewing; she has also recognised the need for information, and feels confident enough to help Anne do some preparatory work for her first specialist appointment.

Health promotion and empowerment are two aspects of care that the staff nurse has recognised as important in her care planning for Anne. These two concepts are inexorably linked and will be discussed here individually, then combined as being essential pre-requisites to the forward movement of health.

There are many definitions of health promotion which is, essentially, an umbrella-term for activity that improves and fosters health. It has been said that health promoters try to influence individuals into making healthier choices (Gott and O'Brien, 1990), but thinking has moved on from this stance and current thought suggests that the term 'health promotion' refers to an approach to care that encompasses a set of values (Maben and Macleod-Clark, 1995) with the overall aim of improving health and preventing disease. They suggest that the values include empowerment, equity, collaboration and participation—all of which are values consistent with humanistic nursing care.

Rodwell (1996) describes empowerment as a helping process, a partnership valuing self and others, involving mutual decision-making, and freedom to make choices and accept responsibility. If we look at the journal entry by the staff nurse, we can see that she had recognised that offering time and attention to Anne was in itself an empowering act, as Anne was able to start working on a brainstorm list that drew out more than was expected. Brainstorming potential solutions can be seen as part of a problem-solving cycle and, as such, this is fundamental to Peplau's model of care which seeks to work collaboratively with patients to find creative solutions to problems. One representation of the problem-solving cycle is seen in *Figure 4.6*.

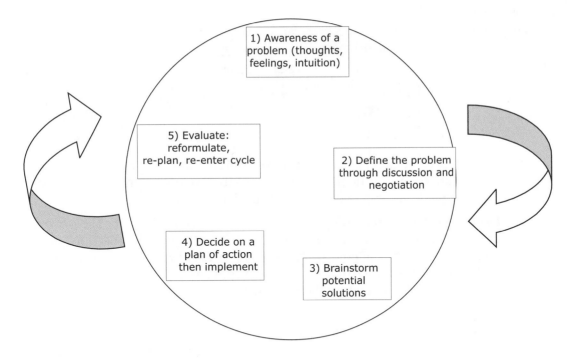

Figure 4.6: Problem-solving cycle

When Anne wrote down a list of potential career options and job opportunities, this activity lay firmly in the third stage of the cycle. Other activities that may be carried out at ward level and also help patients to start to decide about change include the following:

- (suitable for patients thinking about cutting down on their drinking) Ask the patient to think about when their drinking is at its most troublesome. Ask them to list these by thinking back to their last few difficult times. The following format may be useful. It has been filled in using an example from a young man who gathers sheep with a gang of shearers, meeting at the fanks (shearing pen) then ending up in the pub:

Troublesome drinking times									
Times	Day	Time	Hours intended	Hours spent	Place	With whom?	£	Units	Consequences
1	Fri	3pm	3	8 or 9	Fanks, then pub	The shearers	£25	35+	Was ill all weekend. Spent all my wages from the shearing
2									

- Ask the patient to then think of his/her most recent trouble-free drinking times and fill in a similar form:

Trouble-free drinking times									
Times	Day	Time	Hours intended	Hours spent	Place	With whom?	£	Units	Consequences
1	Sun	12 noon	3	3	Sister's	Family	–	6	None—we had Sunday lunch, I drank wine with the meal and a can of beer afterwards. Very pleasant.

- The patient can then be encouraged to consider plans that avoid drinking at work, as they are clearly difficult occasions, and that involve drinking with people who are going to be supportive of any change decisions he makes.

- *Drinking rules and rewards.* Ask the patient to start thinking about his own individual drinking rules, and to think about how he can reward himself for maintaining them. This will be covered in more detail in *Chapter 7*, but involves suggestions, such as the patient not drinking during the day, or not drinking alone. The rules are individual, and will relate to their actual problems as identified in *Part 2* of the problem-solving cycle.

- Ask the patient to fill in some simple questionnaires that aim to increase the awareness of problem drinking. Often when a patient comes into contact with healthcare for the first time with an alcohol-related problem, it may be that they had not considered their problem drinking at all in the past. Some patients will be ready to start thinking about change immediately, but rely on very basic information as a starting point. A questionnaire such as this serves to identify learning needs and to be a trigger for early discussion (Robertson and Heather, 1990):

TRUE   FALSE

1. Abuse of alcohol causes as much damage in society as heroin and other hard drugs

2. Alcohol is a stimulant drug

3. Alcohol will warm you up on a cold day

4. Alcohol can kill you by stopping breathing

5. Alcohol spreads through your body slowly

6. Only the liver removes alcohol from the blood

7. Alcohol contains:
    - Protein
    - Carbohydrates
    - Vitamins

8. How long does it take your body to get rid of the alcohol in 2 pints of beer?
    1. 2 hours
    2. 3 hours
    3. 4 hours

9. You can sober up by:
    - Drinking lots of black coffee
    - Taking a cold shower
    - Getting some fresh air

10. Alcohol can affect the vitamin balance in the body

11. In two pints of beer there are:
    - 150 calories
    - 350 calories
    - 550 calories

12. Drinking spirits is more dangerous than beer

ANSWERS:

1. False. It causes more damage. 2. False. It is a depressant drug. 3. False. It takes heat away. 4. True. But only after drinking very large amounts, rapidly. 5. False. It takes only a few minutes. 6. True. That's why the liver gets overworked if you drink too much. 7. No. No. No. 8. Four hours. 9. All false. 10. True. It gives you nutritional problems. 11. 550. 12. False. Half a pint of ordinary beer is as strong as one pub measure of spirits

Summary

This chapter has explored two of the fundamental concepts of nursing (empowerment and health promotion), and has placed them squarely within the humanistic framework proposed as the means of care delivery in different clinical settings, for those patients who present with alcohol-related problems and who are on the point of considering change . It has also proposed the use of some simple tools to use as a focus within a problem-solving cycle, and that will also help to clarify misconceptions and beliefs within the patient

References

Atkins S, Murphy K (1993) Reflection: a review of the literature. *J Adv Nurs* **18**(8): 1188–92

Baldwin S (1991) Helping the unsure. In: Davidson R, Rollnick S, MacEwan I, eds. *Counselling Problem Drinkers*. Routledge, London

Gott M, O'Brien M (1990) Attitudes and beliefs in health promotion. *Nurs Stand* **5**(2): 30–32

Maben J, Macleod-Clark J (1995) Health promotion: a concept analysis. *J Adv Nurs* **22**(6): 1158–65

Menzies I (1970) *The Functioning of Social Systems as a Defence against Anxiety*. Tavistock, London: (pamphlet number 5)

Miller WR (1983) Motivational interviewing with problem drinkers. *Behav Psychother* **11**: 147–72

Paterson J, Zderad L (1988) *Humanistic Nursing*. National League for Nursing, New York

Peplau HE (1988) *Interpersonal Relations in Nursing*, 2nd edn. Macmillan, Basingstoke

Raistrick D (1991) Helping those who want to change. In: Davidson R, Rollnick S, MacEwan I, eds. *Counselling Problem Drinkers*. Routledge, London

Reynolds W, Scott B (1999) Empathy: a crucial component of the helping relationship. *J Psychiatr Ment Health Nurs* **6**: 363–70

Robertson I, Heather N (1990) *Breaking the Habit: Cutting Down*. Health Education Board for Scotland (HEBS), Edinburgh

Rodwell C (1996) An analysis of the concept of empowerment. *J Adv Nurs* **23**: 305–13

Simpson H (1991) *Peplau's Model in Action*. Macmillan, Basingstoke

Velleman R (1992) *Counselling for Alcohol Problems*. Sage, London

5
Planning for change:
Nursing those in determination

This will address the issues surrounding a patient in the determination stage of change who, having decided that he has a problem, wants to know what he can do about it? It will focus on the nurse's role in helping the patient to make appropriate treatment choices based on whether s/he is opting for controlled drinking, or abstinence. Practical tools, such as time management diaries, will be illustrated and discussed.

At the end of this chapter, the reader will be:

- Familiar with the stage of determination
- Understand the processes involved in planning for change
- Have some idea of the type of resource that can be used in the clinical setting to help patients plan their intended action.

The determination stage of change has been described as a period of preparation. Having moved through the contemplation stage and resolved their ambivalence with a positive decision, patients are keen to move forward. At this time, significant steps may be taken. For instance, those patients who may have reached this stage unassisted may be feeling 'sick of being sick' and want something immediately. One patient who fitted that category was David, a 49-year-old man who had been drinking solidly since his daughter died some seven years previously. He says this of reaching determination:

'I just knew the time was right. I looked around me and I saw that everyone had gone—it's not as if I didn't know they'd given up on me—I was aware at the time, but then nothing seemed to matter. I sort of woke up, it's hard to describe really, I woke up and realised that I had a choice—either carry on like this, or do something. I'd been thinking about it for a while, but it seemed easier to drink somehow. Then it just didn't seem right any more, I wanted my life back—if I couldn't have my daughter, I wanted me. That's why I phoned [the specialist unit]…'

Patients who reach determination via the medium of a supportive relationship with a carer or helper tend to be more in touch with some of the issues about their drinking and changes they need to make because they have carried out the groundwork in advance. For example, they have become aware of the nature of their drinking and the dangers they were facing, and have made an active change decision. Other patients who have had access to a range of self-help materials may also have a deep sense of self-awareness related to the drinking choices they were previously making. The following case study is an example that falls into this category:

* * * * *

Case study 7

Jane is a 40-year-old woman who is training to be a primary school teacher. She lives with her teen-age children, and her mum and dad visit her regularly. She has been working as a classroom assistant since her divorce some three years ago and has one more assignment to complete before she qualifies. When she was first referred to the CPN for advice and counselling, Jane was drinking some 40–45 units of alcohol per week and felt that she could reduce to 14 units, but was not sure which approach would be the most appropriate. Jane knew that she would not succeed if she tried it with no support, but at the same time felt that Alcoholics Anonymous could not help her situation, as she was aware that they advocated an abstinence approach, which was not what she wanted. While waiting for her first appointment, Jane had looked up some self-help resources on the internet and came to the session armed with printouts, and with a drinking diary that the CPN had sent her with the appointment letter that she had now filled in.

It is evident from Jane's history that she is in the determination stage of her change decisions, and is ready to prepare her plan of action. This is in a threshold, and is transitory in nature, as once a decision has been made patients tend to want to move on quickly. It is rewarding when working with patients who are so positive and optimistic about their future, and who are ready to make the lifestyle changes necessary to maintain motivation and determination. One of the key roles of the nurse is to help such patients feel comfortable about their choices, and to help them to develop their own resources to carry them out.

* * * * *

The following is a transcript from the supervision session between the CPN and her line manager:

CPN: *She was certainly armed with enough knowledge. I was quite taken aback when I saw the things that she had downloaded from the net.*

S: Was any of it appropriate?

CPN: *Most of it was very useful, I have to admit. I did advocate caution, though, as there were some diaries that I felt were more like mood diaries, and I didn't get the sense that she was depressed at all. But I did say how pleased I was that she had gone to all the trouble, and that it showed willing.*

S: What did you suggest?

CPN: *I helped her to sort out what would be helpful in the here and now, and then we drew up a timetable between us. The biggest difficulty that she had was in choosing her rewards, as I felt that she was the kind of person who was good at praising others, but not at recognising her own achievements.*

S: And is this important here, do you think?

CPN: *Absolutely. I wanted her to feel that there would be some reinforcement of her change decisions that would encourage her to continue even if some weeks were going to be difficult. I was also keen that she could develop her problem-solving skills to deal with any potential hiccups and didn't feel that would happen if she had just used the leaflets.*

* * * * *

Within the supervision session, the CPN has been able to acknowledge that the patient is an expert in her own drinking behaviour, and at the same time acknowledge her own role as facilitator in the process of the patient exploring her own expertise. She has accepted that Jane has gone to a lot of trouble to find out as much as she can from different sources, such as the internet, and has acted in a supportive way when helping her to sort out which of the leaflets are going to be helpful.

The CPN structured the session with Jane in a way that would help her to logically work through some of the issues surrounding her choice. The first step was to review her drinking diary to identify troublesome drinking times (see *Jane's Drinking Diary, Page 56*).

This diary has raised several important issues for Jane that the medium of a nurse-patient relationship is more likely to help her to address than by working by herself. In the first instance, she is surprised at the amount of units she is drinking, having previously underestimated them. Within the one-to-one session between the CPN and Jane, the CPN was able to help Jane to clarify the number of units of alcohol that she was drinking, and perhaps more importantly the pattern of her consumption, in a non-judgmental way. Velleman (1992) argues that this process not only raises patients' awareness of their drinking pattern, but it also helps them begin to take control of their own situation. Jane has already demonstrated that she is more than capable of doing this in her planning and preparation for this setting, but she may not believe she is able to take control of her drinking so readily given the fact that she has discovered she is drinking more than she at first realised.

Day	What did I drink?	Were there any difficulties?	Units	Total (Units and Cost)
Mon	Wine after work—just over ½ a bottle	None	5	5 £3.50
Tues	Wine after work—the rest of yesterday's plus a glass from a new bottle	I wanted to have another glass, but restrained myself. Had a bit of a craving while I was doing some marking in the evening	6	6 £4.70
Wed	1) 2 Bacardi's in the pub with colleagues 2) rest of wine at home	My mates wanted me to stay but I went home. Am disappointed that I drank the rest of the wine as well.	2 7	9 Units £3
Thurs	Wine after work. I bought a 3 litre box to last the weekend	No	9	£15.20
Fri	Wine after work (from the box)	No	9	
Sat	Glass of wine with my lunch, then a couple in the evening while I was watching Casualty (from the box)	No	9	
Sun	2 Glasses of wine with my lunch, then I finished the box off in the evening.	No	9	
Total for week:			56	£26.40
Any comments about this week? Any questions for the CPN? Please feel free to write whatever you think is important and we will use this as a starter for our discussion.	I was very surprised that I drank so many units. I genuinely thought that my drinking was between 40 and 45 units in a week, and look, it is closer to 56. Does this mean I have underestimated my consumption, and will this pose problems? I did not expect to have cravings, that was a shock— I suspect I always do but I just didn't call them that. I wonder if the box was a bad idea? I could not really measure it as well as I do with bottles.			

Figure 5.1: Jane's drinking diary: determination stage

The CPN decided to share with Jane some information that she had about controlled drinking, with the intention of raising Jane's confidence in her ability to achieve it. It emerged that Jane had retrieved some of this data from the internet, but had found it a little confusing in the format in which it had been presented, but the CPN's table was a little clearer:

Those people who are more likely to achieve a successful outcome in controlled drinking are:

- Those who choose controlled drinking
- Those who are younger
- Those in employment
- Those with a family around them
- Those with a shorter history of abuse
- Those with less physical, emotional or social harm from their drinking
- Those with lower consumption before coming for help
- Those showing no sign of physical dependence.

(Heather and Robertson, 1983)

As part of the planning stage that is determination, the CPN used this list to talk through in detail with Jane, with the intention of clarifying any concerns that she had. Jane automatically fulfils the criteria inherent in the first four categories, as can be seen from her case study. Until the CPN had met Jane, she did not have a clear idea of how long the drinking had been a problem, but according to the history Jane gave her, it had been since the divorce some three years previously. As there appeared to be no withdrawal symptoms or physical damage from the drinking, the CPN was able to reassure Jane that she fitted into the criteria for successful controlled drinking as described above. Jane asked about whether or not cravings constituted dependence. The CPN was able to use her expert knowledge to reassure Jane that although cravings were part and parcel of the dependence syndrome, in isolation from any other symptom of dependence, they cannot be seen as indicative of the condition.

A practical issue that emerged for Jane related to the medium in which she took her alcohol. Buying a wine box is a sound financial idea, as she was able to secure a discount. However, as Jane rightly pointed out, she was unable to moderate her consumption in the same way as with a bottle because she could not physically see the level going down. For many patients this is irrelevant, because most patients measure their drink out in a specific glass and count the number of glasses that they consume. As Jane is in determination, and the actual programme of controlled drinking has technically not yet started, this is a useful insight for the development of her programme. She chose 21 units a week for her first two weekly targets, and stated specifically that it would be bottled wine for this very reason. Controlled drinking is dealt with in more detail in *Chapter 7*.

Figure 5.2 is the care plan that the CPN developed to help Jane to plan for the next stage of change:

Date: <u>00/00</u>

Stage of change: Determination

Phase of the nurse-patient relationship: Identification

Level of intervention: Substance

Partners in Jane's care: *Jane, CPN*

Objective: 1)   To help Jane to prepare for controlled drinking

<u>CARE PLAN</u>

1)   Jane will use a new drinking diary with a weekly target of

21 units, to be reviewed in 2 weeks.

2)   Jane will use bottled wine instead of boxed.

3)   Jane will complete a cravings diary.

4)   The CPN will compile an action folder for Jane, with diaries,

check lists, and blank rewards sheets, to be reviewed and

completed with Jane in the next session.

Review date:

Signature:

Figure 5.2: Care plan: Determination

* * * * *

Case Study 8

Jonathon is a 29-year-old graphic designer whose partner is soon to give birth to their first child. He has been drinking four cans of strong cider a night, plus a bottle of wine at weekends, and feels that he needs to change his drinking behaviour before the baby is born. He only appreciated that he had a problem doing so by himself when he was away for two nights on a work assignment and felt agitated in the evening when he had nothing to drink. His initial motivation was financial, as the alcohol was expensive, but this had developed more into a health concern when he realised that he was drinking three times the recommended limits for a week. He was referred to a specialist alcohol problems clinic, where he was seen by the senior staff nurse.

At Jonathon's first appointment, he said that before he could talk to the nurse he needed to ask if the conversation they had would be recorded in detail, and if anybody else would have access to his notes. The staff nurse explained the unit's confidentiality policy, which meant that, as named nurse, she would keep the case-notes, only sharing them with her supervisor for audit purposes, and with the team doctor should there be a medical issue that needed addressing. She also pointed out to Jonathon that at the end of the interview she would be writing a letter to his GP outlining the care that they had planned.

As the care delivered within the unit was structured around Peplau's model (Peplau, 1988), the staff nurse felt that in this instance she was being placed firmly in the role of counsellor by the patient. He was seeking reassurance about the unit's policy and this appeared to be a stumbling block to a progression towards talking about his problems and to creative problem-solving. The staff nurse knew that in her nursing capacity she could not act as professional counsellor and instead adopted active listening skills in which she reflected back his concerns, reframing them as questions. Using empathy, she communicated her understanding of his concerns at a feelings level and expressed the thought that she too would be wary of opening up in similar circumstances. This is entirely congruent with humanistic nursing principles that advocate a human dialogue and that supports responsible choosing, sharing of self, knowledge and experience (Paterson and Zderad 1988). This enabled Jonathon to open up about his worries and explain why he was initially cautious.

He had been drinking more than he had admitted to his partner, and was experiencing withdrawal symptoms. He had come to the decision by himself tht he wanted to make changes, but wanted complete abstinence not controlled drinking. He had read about this in a journal and had talked to a friend who had undergone a detoxification with the help of a GP. He knew it was likely that he would need medication, but was not sure about whether to tell his partner because he did not want her to worry as she is pregnant. The staff nurse then outlined some options, asking him to decide for himself which he felt was the most appropriate or add to them if he felt appropriate. These were as follows, with rationale:

- *Maintain the status quo*. Jonathon could choose to continue as he is doing, making no changes. In acknowledging this as a valid option, the nurse is accepting Jonathon's expertise in his own drinking, and his own understanding of the level of distress that he is experiencing, and whether it is bearable. Baldwin (1991) identifies the following as reasons for 'no change':
    - The purpose for change has not been made clear
    - Non-involvement in planning [on the part of the patient]
    - No reason to change
    - Costs too high/rewards too low
    - Fear of failure
    - The nurse [counsellor] has not conferred sufficient value and respect for the patient's [client's] existing knowledge
    - Lack of trust between nurse and patient [counsellor and client]
    - Poor communication between the two

- *Starting a controlled drinking programme.* Jonathon has already said that this is not for him, but it needs to be acknowledged as an option that remains open

- *Starting a detoxification programme.* These are discussed in more detail in *Chapter 6*, but essentially involve a period of managed withdrawal from alcohol to a state of abstinence, usually using medication. They are carried out in the community (as either an outpatient, day patient, or at home) or as an inpatient (in a variety of settings, such as a specialist unit, psychiatric unit, or even general hospital settings). This might be appropriate as Jonathon has disclosed he is experiencing withdrawal symptoms.

* * * * *

One issue not addressed in the presented options is the involvement of his partner. This is a transcript of a reflective practice session between the staff nurse and her supervisor that homed in on this aspect of care as it arose, and in the choice that Jonathon made:

Supervise = S: Staff Nurse = SN

S: Do you think that you influenced his choice?

SN: *How do you mean?*

S: Well, he said he wasn't sure that he wanted his partner involved, and yet he seemed to agree readily to home detox [ification] with her involvement?

SN: *Aye, he did. I think that I had some influence, because I presented the options as I saw them in a non-directive way, but was able to guide him through the maze of choice. Every time he spoke about a difficulty with a particular choice, I helped him to see the merits in it and the drawbacks as I saw them, and invited him to put his two penneth in. When we came to whether or not his partner should be involved, he made the decision for himself.*

S: How?

SN: *He spoke about how she was bright and strong, and how she had helped him with difficult things in the past. How she probably knew how his drinking was affecting him any way, and how she would probably prefer to be involved rather than left out. I also told him that those patients undergoing home detox [ification] who have someone helping them with their medication and controlling the home environment seem to do better, and that in a study I read those patients who were cared for with family involvement seemed to remain sober for longer.*

* * * * *

The study that the staff nurse was referring to was by Mirabeau (1997), which suggested that there was a strong association between family involvement and sobriety at three-month follow-up. The implication is that nurses have a critical role in educating both patients and families. In using reflective practice as a supervision tool, the staff nurse has been able to identify her role in Jonathon's decision-making—namely that she helped to clarify concepts for him. The care plan that she drew up with Jonathon is shown on *Page 61* (*Figure 5.3*), and is reflective of the determination stage as a time for planning:

Note that in the partners for Jonathon, the nurse has included the unit's pharmacist. This is an acknowledgement that when a person has an outpatient detoxification and will be attending the unit on a daily basis, the pharmacist plays a role in the monitoring and dispensing of medication. Patients picking up their daily medication from the dispensary often develop a good rapport with the staff, all of which contributes to the overall experience of the patient. The pharmacy staff also have a key role in patient information with regards to medication management.

Date: <u>00/00</u>

Stage of change: Determination

Phase of the nurse-patient relationship: Identification

Level of intervention: Substance

Partners in Jonathon's care: *Jonathon, 'J', Staff Nurse, Unit Doctor, Pharmacist.*

Objective: 1) To help Jonathon to prepare for detoxification

<u>CARE PLAN</u>

1)   Staff nurse and Jonathon to meet with J. on 00/00 in order to discuss the

process involved in detox, and the expected care pathway.

2)   Staff nurse to provide Jonathon with information leaflets for families and

carers, so that J can read them before the next session.

3)   Staff nurse to negotiate a prescription in advance with the unit

doctor ready for start date.

4)   Jonathon to spend this week coordinating with J. over their work contracts, so

that he will have less work to complete during the chosen detox week.

Review date:

Signature:

Figure 5.3: Care plan: Determination

Summary

Within this chapter the importance of planning has been emphasised as the over-riding principle in dealing with the determination stage of change. Any plan that is developed with the patient needs to specify the limits to that change—in Jane's case, the initial plan was to reduce to 21 units, for instance. In Jonathon's, it was to prepare for complete detoxification. The actual planned change will be discussed in the next two chapters in more detail, with detailed plans specific to the chosen action.

One of the challenges for this stage of change lies within family involvement. Raistrick (1991) talks about therapies that change the expectation of alcohol, such as the aversion therapies. It must be argued that expectations within the family will also change, and therefore their involvement if possible at this crucial stage will go a long way towards preventing any misconceptions by either party. For instance, spouses may be surprised that trust does not return readily after the problematic drinking stops: preparing them for this eventuality will avoid any sense of anti-climax after their partner's detoxification. One of the roles of the nurse in this instance is to act as resource person for all consenting parties within the family unit, while respecting the wishes and confidentiality of the patient.

References

Baldwin S (1991) Helping the unsure. In: Davidson R, Rollnick S, MacEwan I, eds. *Counselling Problem Drinkers.* Routledge, London

Heather N, Robertson I (1983) *Controlled Drinking*, 2nd edn. Methuen, London

Mirabeau F (1997) Evaluation outcome study of family education in the treatment of alcoholic patients. *J Addict Nurs* **9**(2): 77–80

Paterson JG, Zderad LT (1988) *Humanistic Nursing*, 2nd edn. National League of Nursing, New York

Peplau HE (1988) *Interpersonal Relations in Nursing*, 2nd edn. Macmillan, Basingstoke

Raistrick D (1991) Helping those who want to change. In: Davidson R, Rollnick S, MacEwan I, eds. *Counselling Problem Drinkers.* Routledge, London

Velleman R (1992) *Counselling for Alcohol Problems.* Sage, London

6

Action stage of change 1: Nursing a patient through detoxification

This chapter will discuss the process of detoxification as provided and delivered using humanistic nursing principles. It takes the case study of two patients in different settings; one in a specialist community service, and one in a general medical. Examples of some of the assessment tools to be found at the end of the book are used here to demonstrate their practical application.

At the end of this chapter, the reader will:

- Have an understanding of the principles and practice of detoxification based on the current knowledge base
- Have an understanding of the action stage of change.

Management of alcohol withdrawal

This chapter will describe in detail the nature of withdrawal symptoms and demonstrate in some depth the care of two patients who had typical yet differing experiences of the withdrawal process. CRAG (1994) highlighted the need for the clinical areas to have specific treatment guidelines, especially given the increase in numbers of patients admitted to general hospitals with alcohol-related problems (Chick *et al*, 1985). The assessment tools used in this chapter form an integral part of a protocol that aims to fulfil the role of such guidelines.

Withdrawal symptoms from alcohol cessation will begin to occur after six to twenty-four hours, dependent upon the intake and metabolism of the individual. Once the blood alcohol level approaches zero, the patient will begin to feel uncomfortable. The overall objective of any intervention at this stage is to facilitate a safe withdrawal period, and a clinical protocol guides nurses and other practitioners into helping to choose the most suitable option to offer their patients. The flow chart (*Figure 6.1*) is one example:

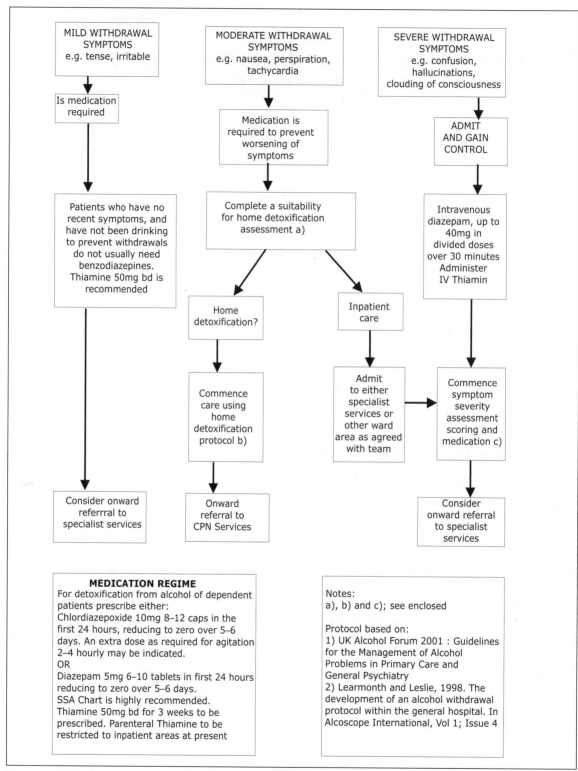

Figure 6.1: Patient presents with a history of alcohol problems, in alcohol withdrawal

The action stage of change

The action stage of change marks a significant step in a patient's motivation and thinking. Cooper (2000) describes this as a vibrant and meaningful time for the patient and it is not difficult to see why. One patient, Anne, said this of reaching action:

> 'It was as though everything that I had wanted for Christmas arrived at once, but I was too terrified to open my presents. We had planned it, yes, but I couldn't imagine no chink clink in the shopping trolley and secretly I didn't think the tablets would really work, but I wasn't going to tell my CPN that, was I? I'd been to AA once; they'd said no pain no gain, but I kept thinking there had been enough pain, hadn't there? And then suddenly, the day arrived, and I reached for the tablets not the gin, and oh, it was ace!'

Smith (1998) described in his findings the problem drinker's lived experience of suffering and found the following rock bottom experiences that finally motivated people in his study to move on from pre-contemplation:

- Fear of public exposure and disgrace
- Private shame
- Physical degradation
- Delirium tremens
- Complete loss of self respect
- Contemplating suicide
- Attempted suicide
- Extreme guilt
- Becoming 'down and out'
- Losing one's purpose and meaning of life

It does not need to be so dramatic. Some patients arrive at a decision before they have experienced such profound difficulties; others have one incident that nudges them to change, such as a shock drink-driving conviction. Either way, patients in action are motivated, determined and usually optimistic about their future. If patients have been in touch with the service beforehand, then planning will have already taken place for the change process, as is the case with the patient in *Case Study 10*.

* * * * *

Case Study 10

David is a 33-year-old man who has been drinking problematically for several years. He described how his drinking pattern used to be that of a binge nature—spending several days in a row drinking more than a bottle of spirits at a time, then spending several weeks abstinent. Since Hogmanay over four months ago, he has been a daily drinker and has noticed that he needs to drink alcohol from early morning as soon as he wakes because otherwise he would have troublesome withdrawal symptoms. He had been considering asking for help, but was spurred into action when he lost his job and a relationship, both due to excessive alcohol consumption.

A referral to the local CPN was made at his request by the GP, and he came to his initial session armed with ideas about detoxification followed by disulfiram therapy to prove he was 'sober and get my job back'. At that stage the CPN assessed him and felt he was in determination, and together they planned a home detoxification which is due to commence today. For the week of detoxification he is staying with his mother.

The period of detoxification referred to in David's case is a managed period during which the patient's withdrawal symptoms are alleviated. An advantage of carrying this out in a health care setting be that home-based, community-based or inpatient-based is that the symptom relief can be monitored closely to ensure that there are no adverse situations occurring. As alcohol is a central nervous system (CNS) depressant, then the withdrawal symptoms tend to be largely related to CNS hyper-excitability. These include:

- Tremor (of the hands, arms, leading to whole body)
- Anxiety
- Sweating
- Muscle jerks
- Hypertension
- Nausea and vomiting
- Anorexia
- Diarrhoea
- Nightmares
- Insomnia
- Epileptic type seizures
- Pyrexia
- Tachycardia
- Depression
- Perceptual disturbance, including hallucinations and illusions

Most patients who have developed alcohol dependence will experience some of these, but few who come into contact with services during the action stage will experience all, as they are being actively managed to reduce the severity of such symptoms. However, it is not unusual to have a person admitted via A&E who is demonstrating the full rage of symptoms, or who is unconscious after having a withdrawal seizure because of unmanaged abstinence (such as running out of alcohol, unplanned). Such situations are treated as a medical emergency because other complications may occur, particularly hyperpyrexia and Wernicke's encephalopathy (see *Introduction*).

If we return to David's case, we learn that he is in a supportive working relationship with a CPN and has spent a session with her planning for this eventuality. Here are:

a) David's alcohol misuse assessment that the CPN completed as part of the orientation phase of the nurse-patient relationship;

b) the assessment checklist that the CPN completed prior to agreeing upon home detoxification;

c) the care plan that the CPN drew up with David; and

d) the progress diary that tracks the week of his detoxification, including the symptom severity assessment chart.

They are presented in this way to demonstrate the practicalities involved in home detoxification, and to highlight the progress of the nurse-patient relationship using Peplau's model of care.

a) **Alcohol Misuse Assessment**
   (Based on Highland Primary Care NHS Trust community assessment tool care pathway)

David's **pathway to assessment and care:**		
Current Assessment	**Named Nurse**	**Date**
Started with	*CPN*	*00/00*
Transferred to:		
Transferred to:		
David's **Details:**		
Name & Title David	CHI number *1234567*	
Address (Inc Telephone) xx	GP (inc telephone) *xx*	
Date of Birth: Age: *33*	Referred by & date: GP on *00/00*	
Next of Kin Name: *Mother, Mrs McB*	Date of first assessment:	*00/00*
Address: *xx*	Reason for referral:	*Assessment and possible Home detoxification*
Telephone: *12345*	Alcometer reading:	*Not assessed —David admits to drinking this morning*

David's **History**

Ask *David* about his **previous** drinking. Questions to include: how old was he when he first drank; when did it first become a problem; were there any precipitating causes; has he been abstinent; if so, how did he achieve this:

David has been drinking since he was 16. He started with his pals after the Summer Dances, and noticed by 18 he was getting drunk every weekend. No obvious precipitants, but David says that he drinks more heavily at festive periods. He has only been sober for a few weeks at a time, triggered by bouts of sickness and possible withdrawal symptoms.

Ask *David* about his recent drinking. Include pattern, quantity, length of recent binges, average units taken per day or week; use diary if possible to help David tell his story:

It seems from David's diary that he is currently drinking approx. 30 units a day, starting on waking to control tremors. He tops up during the day, never being intoxicated. He is drinking average strength malt whisky and avoids the pub and other drinkers. He was hiding his drink in a vacuum flask at work, but was caught out.

Social information:

Nationality:	✓British	✓ Other — please specify	Ethnicity:	✓White	✓ Other — please specify
Language Needs:	English ✓	Gaelic ✓	Other — please specify		Interpreter? *No*
Lives with: *Alone*	Type of accommodation: *Local Authority*		Marital status: *Single*		Children: *None*

Summary of David's background

David was born and brought up in a small town by the coast. He has 3 sisters, none of whom have an alcohol problem. His father died 2 years ago, and he feels he has grieved appropriately. He does not attribute his heavy drinking to this event. There seem to be no mental health problems in the immediate family, although he says an uncle has been depressed for some time and sees a CPN.

He has lost his job, and has no current relationship. There are no debts at present, but he is aware that resources are the lowest they have been, and unless he stops drinking and starts work again he will not be able to pay a credit card bill. He has never been in trouble with the police because of his drinking or for any other reason.

Previous and current withdrawal symptoms			
PREVIOUS		**CURRENT**	
☐ None	☐ N/A	☐ None	
✓ Sweating	✓ Anxiety	✓ Sweating	☐ Anxiety
☐ Low mood	☐ Diarrhoea	☐ Low mood	☐ Diarrhoea
☐ Hallucinations	✓ Sleep disturbance	☐ Hallucinations	✓ Sleep disturbance
✓ Vomiting	☐ Seizures	☐ Vomiting	☐ Seizures
✓ Nausea	✓ Tachycardia	☐ Nausea	✓ Tachycardia
☐ Agitation	✓ Tremor	☐ Agitation	✓ Tremor
☐ Other (specify)		☐ Other (specify)	

Has *David* ever been in contact with services for this before? If so please give details of detoxification history and treatment used (e.g. medication, counselling):	
David has been to see his GP on one occasion, who referred him here. There has been no other contact and no prescribing.	
Does *David* have any current or past medical problems, eg. diabetes, epilepsy, heart conditions? Please give details including medication.	*David has no history of medical problems other than childhood complaints.*

Outcome of *David's* Assessment: include stage of change.

David appears motivated to change and I would assess him as being in determination today. This is evidenced by him having a clear idea that he wants to stop drinking, and he is looking for guidance on how to achieve his aims. I have discussed options with him and will assess his home situation for suitability for home detoxification. He has signed the community detoxification agreement[1].

Subjective observations:

> *1. David appears anxious today, a little edgy*

> *2. David appears keen to move on and change his drinking*

Objective observation

> *a) David is in mild withdrawals*

Signature: CPN
Signature: *David*

The assessment tool is a core specialist assessment that focusses on the patient's history and in particular the drinking problems with which he has presented. This tool was developed in

---

1   See *Chapter 10* — resource file.

this format to serve one major function. It provides a core care package that follows the patient's pathway through care and should any situation arise that might involve him entering another service for a period of time, the assessment and care plans will travel with him. Should David develop delirium tremens, for example, if his withdrawals are not responding to the prescribed medication, then it is likely he will be admitted to the local unit. As the staff from both the community and the inpatient areas were responsible for developing the assessment tool, it is designed in a format that will gather the necessary information for both parties and negate the need for repeating the questions, especially if he is unwell. The intention is that the assessment follows him back to the community.

b) Assessment of suitability for home detoxification

This was completed by the CPN in what became the identification phase of the nurse-patient relationship and formed part of the planning session with David; it constitutes part of the Trust's detoxification protocol (see *Figure 6.2*). A copy of this is kept with the nursing documentation for audit purposes and for future reference should he ever re-present. David answered this from the perspective of a potential stay at his mother's home. Had he been by himself, his score would have been much reduced:

Such a tool is a useful guide to whether or not a patient could do well at home, or whether an alternative arrangement will be more suitable. Note how it was personalised, a factor that helps patients to feel that they are an integral part of the planning of care. This particular assessment tool is based on the guidelines as laid out by the UK Alcohol Forum (2001). During the planning meeting, the tool became a prompt for meaningful interaction between David and his CPN; by expanding on some of the questions in discussion, David was able to recognise factors that have influenced his drinking to date. For instance, in considering question IV (noise), he realised that at home there are footsteps from the flat upstairs and from the common landing every evening and often into the night. This he believed would have caused him to feel agitated—the last time he tried to stop drinking by himself, the noise level in the evening had led to him shouting at a neighbour for slamming a door, then reaching for a drink 'to calm down'. When the detoxification period is coming to a close the CPN will prepare David for the maintenance stage of change by looking at the triggers to drinking and the consequences of succumbing; noisy neighbours are likely to be on the list.

Does David have a history of:

1.	Withdrawal fits	Yes—	No✓?
2.	Psychosis	Yes—	No✓?
3.	Current medical problems, including hypertension	Yes—	No✓?
4.	Suicidal ideation	Yes—	No✓?

If yes to any of the above, take history and discuss with GP.

Home environment suitability for detoxification		**Score as directed:**
Availability of supporter	Always	3
	Often	2✓
	Sometimes	1
	Never	0
Attitude of supporter	Very supportive	3✓
	Supportive	2
	Slightly supportive	1
	Not supportive	0
Commitment supporter	Very committed	3✓
	Committed	2
	Slightly committed	1
	Not committed	0
Level of noise	Tranquil	3
	Reasonably quiet	2✓
	Noisy	1
	Very noisy	0
Presence of drinkers	Never	3✓
	Sometimes present	2
	Often present	1
	Always present	0
	TOTAL SCORE	<u>13</u>
Date Completed	Signed	

If the score is 6 or below, evaluate with David's family to try to bring the score up (e.g. negotiate a 'no alcohol in the house' rule during the period of detoxification

Figure 6.2: Assessment of suitability for home detoxification

c) David's detoxification care plan

Name	*David*	**Key Worker:** *CPN*

Stage of Change	*Action*
Level of Intervention	*Substance*
Phase of nurse-patient relationship	*Action*
Partners in David's care	*David, Mum, CPN, GP*
Objective	*For David to achieve abstinence by safe detoxification*

Date:

1. David has agreed to stay at his mum's for the week of detoxification

2. CPN has agreed to monitor David's progress using a hand-held care plan which will stay at David's home

3. David has agreed to all monitoring as listed on his assessment checklist, including alcometer recording and BP recording

4. CPN will liase with GP to prescribe medication; chlordiazepoxide the drug of choice in this practice area, in addition to thiamine

REVIEW DATE: **SIGNED:**

Figure 6.3: Care Plan, Home Detoxification (Action)

It will be noted from David's care plan above that reference to a hand-held care plan has been made. This refers to the documentation that will stay in the home with David and prevents repetition. Because the CPN will be visiting twice on the first two days of detoxification and daily thereafter if all is going to plan, there are going to be several observations to record. It makes sense that the detoxification recordings are held together in a folder that will then be placed in the patient's nursing notes. Thus the assessment documentation and checklist will be held with the main care plan at the CPN base. At home, the medication chart, symptom severity assessment sheet, the carer support pack, a progress diary and a patient information sheet form what has now become a hand-held care plan.

d) Daily Progress Diary

This records David's progress during his detoxification period. It has many uses and, in particular, because patients are in charge of looking after it and therefore have access to it at all times, they are being active partners in care. This is an essential component in humanistic nursing, in which human beings are considered free and are expected to be involved in their own care and decisions involving them (Paterson and Zderad, 1988).

This is the diary completed over a period of five days. The SSA score refers to an assessment that the CPN carried out using the attached Symptom Severity Assessment form. This converts withdrawal symptoms into a numerical score from which the dosage of medication is calculated, and the one illustrated here was developed by the substance misuse team in Highland region. Its use is most appropriate in inpatient settings, as it relies on scoring the patient four times a day: clearly it is the normal scenario that a CPN will only visit twice in the first instance. However, the score is a validated, objective tool that can inform practice and assist in more accurate control of symptoms. There are several other versions available, and most specialist units have developed their own variation. The CPN visited David's GP to arrange for the prescription in advance, and the diazepam was dispensed with 'As prescribed' labelling: this allows dispensing according to the symptoms as negotiated between David, the CPN and the GP.

Diary including Daily Record of Medication

This is a record for you to fill in to let the CPN know what you have taken, and when. There is also space for you to write down any comments, for instance, if you feel sleepy, or if you felt that your symptoms were not well controlled. We would like your partner or next of kin to help you with this chart, as they may notice something, which you do not.

Name: David
Detox started on:............. CPN:............ CPN Telephone Number

Day	Medication	Morn 8am	Lunch 12 noon	Tea 6pm	Bed 10pm	Comments	Supporter initials
Mon	Diazepam	15mg	10mg	10mg	10mg	D: *I took the 3 tabs first thing, but they made me a bit sleepy. I didn't feel sick, just a bit queasy. I was a bit shaky today.* CPN: *SSA 7 @ 9am. SSA 6 @5pm. See chart. Advised 10mg for tomorrow am before my visit. May have 5mg extra tonight if D needs it.*	
	Thiamine	50mg		50mg			
Tue	Diazepam	10mg	5mg	5mg	10mg	D: *I had a good night, I was so surprised.* CPN: *SSA 4 at 9.30am. Advised re diet and fluids as he had not eaten very much yesterday. SSA 4 at 5pm. Advised 10mg for bedtime dose.*	
	Thiamine	50mg		50mg			
Wed	Diazepam	5mg	2mg	2mg	5mg	D: *Feeling OK, really. Better than I thought. No more shakes, just a bit edgy.* Mum: *David wants to start the tablets he talked about. When will that be?* CPN: *SSA 2 at 9.30am. Will not return this afternoon unless David rings. See chart. Explained to David and Mum that he can start Disulfiram on Friday if he wants to. Will arrange script & warning card.*	
	Thiamine	50mg		50mg			
Thur	Diazepam	2mg	0	0	2mg	David: *I want to go to my sister's today. Will that be ok?* CPN: *SSA 0 at 9.15 am. Advised to take 2mg tonight as a last dose. Advised that David is free to go wherever he wants so long as he feels up to it and doesn't drink alcohol.*	
	Thiamine	50mg		50mg			
Fri	Thiamine Disulfiram	50mg 400mg		50mg		CPN: *Talked through the implications and practicalities of being on Disulfiram[2].*	

Figure 6.4: Medication Diary

As can be seen from the diary, David had a very uneventful withdrawal period. His symptoms were well controlled by the diazepam regime and he needed fairly low doses of sedation. The CPN filled in the following reflections in her reflective practice journal that demonstrated some of the theory underpinning her practice, and also demonstrated a level of self awareness about the philosophy underpinning it:

---

2   Disulfiram: see *Chapter 9*

	MONDAY		TUESDAY			WEDNESDAY	THURSDAY	FRIDAY
Date								
Time:	8	1	8	1	6	8	8	8
Pulse	2	2	1	1	1	0	0	0
Tremor	1	1	1	1	1	1	0	0
Perspiration	2	1	1	1	0	0	0	0
Anxiety	1	1	1	1	1	1	0	0
Agitation	1	1	0	0	1	0	0	0
Perceptual disturbance	0	0	0	0		0	0	0
Orientation	0	0	0	0		0	0	0
Blood Pressure:	140/85	140/85	140/80	140/80		130/80	120/70	130/70
Total	7	6	4	4	4	2	0	0

Date						
Time	8	1	6	10		
Pulse						
Tremor						
Perspiration						
Anxiety						
Agitation						
Perceptual disturbance						
Orientation						
Blood Pressure:						
Total						

Ward: Name: Unit number: Consultant:

PULSE:
79 or below	0
80-99	1
100-119	2
120 or over	3

TREMOR:
No Tremor	0
Tremor of outstretched hand	1
Constant tremor of arms	2
Whole body tremor	3

PERSPIRATION:
None	0
Moist skin	1
Beads of sweat	2
Profuse sweating	3

ANXIETY
None	0
Understandable anxiety	1
Anxiety and panics	2
Constant panic	3

AGITATION
None	0
Restlessness	1
Can't remain seated	2
Constantly restless	3

PERCEPTUAL DISTURBANCE
None	0
Illusion/fleeting hallucination	1
Formed hallucinations	2
Vivid hallucinations	3

ORIENTATION
Correct	0
Uncertain of date	1
Date wrong more than 2 days	2
Time and place wrong	3

DIAZEPAM
Score	
0-1	No Medication
2-3	2mg
4-5	5mg
6-7	10mg
8-10	15mg
over 10	20mg

David was an ideal candidate for home detox [ification] because he had none of the contra-indications. There was no evidence of confusion, suicidal ideas, no history of fits, he wasn't a drug user, in fact he had a near perfect score on the suitability scoring sheet. I wanted him to feel that he was in control of what was happening to him, because he had not been in control of very much recently. He'd lost control of his drinking, and he'd lost his job, and he had no relationship because of his drinking. I felt that if he were effectively in charge, he would feel empowered, then I would just be a partner in his care. It is hard to let go sometimes; the urge is to take charge of the assessment because I think that's what some patients really want; me to be the expert nurse and them to be the patient, but I knew that David was motivated and determined and ready for feeling different. In some cases I feel that we go along to patients' homes armed with all this equipment, the sphyg, the Alcometer, the stethoscope, and we are expected to measure all these physical symptoms and calculate their medication—it's all science, and the art gets lost. I think that's why I am glad that we use Peplau's model because she said that nursing is a helping art. The medium of this art is the intuition and resourcefulness, the process is the way we interact with our patients and the product in this case was David being whole, being sober, not needing to reach for his booze in the morning. I sometimes need to see the product to remind me of the process and the medium. In fact, my reading goal for this week is going to be a refresher on Peplau's model.

The next patient, as with David, was also in the Action stage of change. However, his situation was quite different as we can see from the following:

* * * * *

Case Study 11

Angus is a 52-year-old tablet controlled diabetic who lives with his wife and two of their four children in a remote rural area. Over the last three years as his alcohol consumption has escalated, he has become unable to control either his drinking or his blood sugar. The diabetic nurse took bloods from him, then initially referred him to the dietician, as she felt his sugars were unstable because he had not been controlling his carbohydrate intake; whilst this was strictly true, it was the fact that he had been getting his carbohydrates from beer that was causing the problem, as it had been difficult for him to manage his diet. When the dietician completed a full dietary assessment she discovered that he was drinking at least 100 units of alcohol a week, and that he was experiencing withdrawal symptoms.

A referral to the CPN was made for an initial specialist assessment as part of the Trust's single shared assessment protocol. This led to prompt action, as when the blood results came back to the diabetic nurse they indicated both liver and kidney damage, with a blood sugar of 26.5. The CPN had already assessed Angus as being in the Action stage of change from her interview, and a decision was made to offer him an inpatient detoxification admission to a local cottage hospital, which he readily accepted.

The following is a copy of the specialist assessment that the CPN completed for Angus. Again it has been completed to demonstrate the practicality of the form. Notice that although this was completed in the same Trust, this is a different assessment tool to the one in the previous case study. This is because he had been referred through a single shared assessment protocol, and the key worker was to remain the diabetic nurse. This assessment tool is a standard form, and is not part of an assessment for home detoxification. When this was completed, a summary was produced, and copies of it distributed, with Angus' permission to the GP, the dietician and the diabetic nurse, to keep with his main case-notes; the advantage of such an approach is that it guarantees continuity of care and again avoids the need for repetition.

CPN(A) Specialist Assessment

PATIENT NAME: **Angus** **DOB** **Age 52**

RECENT DRINKING HISTORY

Day & Date	Amount:	Approx. Units	Comments:
Mon 7th	? 8 pints beer, 4 tots	20	In the pub with friends
Tues 8th	? 8 or 9 pints	18	In the pub with friends
Wed 9th	? 8 or 9 pints	18	In the pub with friends
Thurs 10th	? 8 or 9 pints	18	In the pub with friends
Fri 11th	? 6 pints + ½ bottle whisky	27	In the pub and at home
Sat 12th	½ bottle whisky	15	At home
Sun 13th	7 pints	14	In the pub with friends

WITHDRAWALS
- Hallucinations?
- Withdrawal seizures?

Angus has sweating and experiences tremors. He is agitated at times, describes himself as bad tempered. Has collapsed twice—he does not know if this is because of his diabetes or if they were seizures. He has had some visual hallucinations; he once thought his dog had a head at each end.

DRINKING AND TREATMENT HISTORY

Angus started drinking when he was 18 and he worked offshore. He would be sober for the two weeks he was on the rig, then he would hit the bar at the airport when the helicopter landed to bring them home. He drank heavily for as long as he was home, but was always sober at work. He then developed health problems that took him away from the rig—became diabetic and had to leave. This was three years ago and he has been a daily drinker ever since. He drinks in the pub, always beer, occasionally has a nip of whisky. He had a lot of money from working offshore, and he felt he could afford this at first, but resources are drying up. He has never sought help before. He experiences strong cravings for alcohol.

FAMILY HISTORY

Born and brought up in (x), his family owned a croft with shares in the common grazings. They are a Gaelic speaking family and all four children were in Gaelic medium education. Angus wanted to get involved in the Feis[3] when he came onshore, but finds he has no motivation. His father and mother are both still alive: neither drink at all, and are both Free Presbyterian. He has four brothers and two sisters, and Angus feels he is the black sheep in the family as he is the only one who drinks.

EMPLOYMENT STATUS

Unemployed. Angus worked offshore as an electrician on the oil rigs until three years ago then took medical redundancy. Currently on incapacity benefit.

FORENSIC HISTORY

No previous problems

Court case pending?   No

ILLICIT DRUG USE

Never used drugs

DEBT

Angus is not in debt, but has requested a benefits review.

PSYCHIATRIC HISTORY

None

MEDICAL HISTORY

1)   Angus is diabetic, diet and tablet controlled

2)   Angus has essential hypertension

CURRENT MEDICATION

Metformin	850mg daily
Atenolol	50mg daily
Frusemide	20mg daily

---

3   Feis—this is a Gaelic cultural group that organises traditional music and Gaelic tuition locally.

STAGE OF CHANGE TODAY, DECISIONS MADE TOGETHER

Angus is in the action stage of change; he says he has had enough of drinking and he wants to stop completely because his health is now suffering. He does not believe that controlled drinking is an option for him, and he describes himself as being an alcoholic. He feels he needs a lot of support to achieve his goal of abstinence, and that without an admission he would be at risk of collapsing again. We have agreed on medical detoxification as a priority and Angus has agreed for me to make a phone call today to discuss this with his key worker before a bed is booked. He has not had a drink today, and is mildly tremulous already; if there is a bed today it would be possible for him to come in now. His wife can bring a bag to the ward later on. Angus has asked for follow up from me [CPN] both during and after a detoxification, as he would like to do some work on his cravings and on ways of spending his time now that he is not working. He would also like someone to speak to his wife.

Signed   <u>CPN</u>   Signed   *Angus*   Date_____

Angus has made a distinct statement about his drinking intentions; he has expressed a clear desire for change, and has asked for some specific input to help him with cravings and time management. The specialist assessment has served to add to the picture being gathered by the diabetic nurse and the dietician, and has given indicators of his commitment to future support. In this situation, he was admitted to the ward straight away and his care was co-ordinated jointly between the staff nurse and the CPN, with input from the diabetic team.

When working in such a partnership, each member has their own expertise to offer. Some of this expertise is overt, such as the role of the diabetic nurse, who will liaise with the ward to monitor Angus' blood sugars and advise on medication. It is likely that his blood sugars will be erratic until his detoxification is finished, as his body will have to adjust to a different diet. The CPN will visit on a daily basis just as if Angus were a home detoxification patient, and will assist the ward team with their nursing management. The staff nurse who is his named nurse will be seen as a contact for all parties, and will be responsible for co-ordinating all aspects of his inpatient nursing care. Using Peplau's model of care, Angus will be involved in this process in its entirety, as during the exploitation phase of the nurse-patient relationship, he is making full use of the resources around him. Simpson (1991) suggests that the patient in this phase seeks more information about his health problem, discusses with other patients to see whether he is getting accurate information and, as he considers his situation, his dependency on the nursing team is readjusted. Herein lies a problem: Angus is being nursed in a cottage hospital in a medical setting. It is unlikely that he will have other patients with an alcohol problem to chat to for him to fulfil this important aspect of achieving health-directed behaviour. In this case, the nursing alliance that is the team will share this role and act as surrogate. Moreover, the staff nurse could offer Angus the chance to have a member of Alcoholics Anonymous visit him on the ward should he so wish, as he did say that he was considering attending when he left.

The nursing care that Angus receives for his alcohol problem is all based on sound evidence, using validated tools. Holmes (1990) believes that there is a dichotomy between the demand for such evidence-based practice and the adoption of humanistic principles. He sets out this dichotomy using the work of Sarvimäki (1988), who argued that thinking in 'general laws' is inappropriate to nursing because each patient is unique and individual. If nurses use 'communicative action', then patients can be helped to exercise control over their own health and health care. He also argues that an emphasis on objectivity prevents the nurse from recognising her patient as a person. The assessment tool and scoring sheets used in Angus's care and those used in other detoxification situations may well appear to be rooted in the scientific base of nursing; however, when the care is delivered using the artistry of humanistic principles, the experience can be rewarding for both patient and nurse.

Returning to Angus's care, the staff nurse who was to be his named nurse admitted him to a side ward, where he would not be disturbed by the comings and goings in the main ward area. She introduced herself, then showed him where the toilet facilities and day room were. However, she noticed that his tremor was quite marked and that he was extremely anxious, so she made a decision to score him using the symptom severity assessment chart straight away. He scored 11 and, as he needed 20mg diazepam as soon as possible to alleviate his symptoms, she called the on-call doctor to sign the prescription. Angus had a difficult two days, as he started vomiting and needed parenteral medication and fluid replacement. He also needed anti-emetic medication and anti-psychotic medication, as he developed clouding of consciousness and some hallucinatory experiences. He had no sleep at all on the first night, and could not have night sedation because of concerns over his blood sugar, so was very tired. The nurses administered intravenous thiamine as prescribed. He did settle well after this and was actively managing his own urinalysis, blood sugar and blood pressure recording as at home by day three.

The staff nurse chose to use a nursing diagnosis care plan for his detoxification management (see *Chapters 3* and *10*), with the rationale that not all of the nursing staff had yet been able to attend the training session on what was then a new detoxification protocol. The advantage of the tool is that it gives clear, concise instructions and is evidence-based, hence it acts as a learning tool for staff. Learmonth and Leslie (1998) found that only 42% of staff in their project group had received any training on alcohol problems, and The Scottish Executive (2002: paragraph 7.23) are recommending that the management of alcohol problems be added to the curriculum for future nurse education. The staff nurse in choosing this course was also acknowledging the fact that her team comprised nurses of different grades, with different levels of skills and expertise. Benner (1984) argued that practice knowledge in the expert nurse is gained over time and with clinical experience; she defined this knowledge in six categories, one of which is 'assumptions, expectations and sets'. The staff nurse was concerned that the unit did not assist in detoxification often enough to develop expertise. Also, because most of the detoxifications they had conducted over recent years had been uncomplicated, then the staff would not necessarily be as prepared for a new situation in which the patient's progress did not run smoothly; they may have assumptions and expectations based on previous experience. Although this was Angus' first detoxification, she predicted some complications based on her knowledge of his diabetes, his hypertension and the SSA score on admission.

This is a section of what became a peer reflective practice discussion between the CPN and the staff nurse. Note how a major function of the discussion served as peer support, and how each nurse shared with the other their own individual expertise.

* * * * *

SN: *I was so glad to see you arrive yesterday! Gosh, I though we might have needed to send him through on the air ambulance for a while, but he did seem to settle, didn't he?*

CPN: Aye, he did. My concern was for his blood sugars, though, I was terrified he'd go into a diabetic coma or something!

SN: *No chance. We had him on 2 hourly BMs[4], and it's not as if he was insulin-dependent or anything. I think it looks as if a lot of his diabetic problems have been precipitated by over eating and over-drinking, and now he seems so motivated to change everything that he's even talking about joining the gym* [laughs].

CPN: Is he really? Gosh, I'll mention that to him if that's OK. One of the aims for us now as he is entering maintenance is to focus on relapse prevention and time management, so that would be a super idea for him. Will he be fit enough?

SN: *You'll have to check his latest ECG. He has really high blood pressure still, and I don't think it would do Angus any good just yet. Could that be the detox, do you think?*

CPN: Possibly. If you look at the International Handbook there's a section by Saunders [1991] that covers the effects of physical complications, and one is systemic hypertension. There's a copy on my desk upstairs. Do we know how long he has had this?

SN: *About five years. Of course, he was drinking heavily then, so that might well explain it.*

CPN: Well, in my experience the blood pressure settles down to a reasonable level by about Day 7 of the detox. However, if he has hypertension anyway, it is likely to be higher than the norm. Can I ask you something else?

SN: *Sure.*

CPN: How do you feel about having nursed Angus through what was really a very difficult two days for him? Now that he's settled and more able, then I guess you must be relieved, but how did you really feel about it when he was confused?

SN: [laughs] *Honest? Well, I was really concerned when the medication didn't seem to be working, and I am glad that you were able to be here with us. To be truthful, though, I think that it was a useful learning experience for the whole team, and it is so nice to see him improving like this. We often get wrapped up in the technicalities of care, the blood pressure recording, the blood sugar, the urinalysis. Yet when he was frightened, one of the nursing assistants just sat with him, quietly, and her presence alone seemed to help. It seemed to me that by that very act alone she was being more caring than any of the technical stuff.*

CPN: You should have a look at Leininger's[5] book—there's a copy in the library—it's about caring, and she says that both the technological stuff and the artistry are components.

* * * * *

4 A form of blood sugar testing using a small monitor and a lance.
5 Leininger MM, ed (1981) *Care: The Essence of Nursing and Health.* Wayne State University Press, Detroit

Summary

What happened between the staff nurse and the CPN became more than just a casual conversation. Benner described such discussions as helping nurses to 'uncover meanings' that are essentially acquired through caring (1984). This demonstrates the value of reflective practice in a general medical setting, where patients in the action stage of change are being cared for in a team with different staff grades and different disciplines. Both David and Angus had successful outcomes to their detoxification and staff in each case were able to reflect on their practice in different ways. The next chapter focusses on the same stage, but covers controlled drinking.

References

Benner P (1984) *From Novice to Expert: Excellence and Powering Clinical Nursing Practice.* Addison-Wesley, Menlo Park, CA

Cooper DB, ed (2000) *Alcohol Problems.* Radcliffe Medical Press, Abingdon

CRAG/SCOTMEG, Working Group on Mental Illness (1994) *The Management of Alcohol Withdrawal and Delirium Tremens: A Good Practice Statement.* HMSO, Edinburgh

Holmes CA (1990) Alternatives to natural science foundations for nursing. *Int J Nurs Stud* **17**(3): 187–98

Learmonth L, Leslie H (1998) The development of an alcohol-withdrawal protocol within the general hospital setting. *Alcoscope Int Rev Alcoholism Man* **1**(4): 12–16

Leininger MM, ed (1984) *Care: The Essence of Nursing and Health.* Wayne State University Press, Detroit

Paterson JG, Zderad LT (1988) *Humanistic Nursing.* National League of Nurses, New York

Sarvimäki A (1988) Nursing care as a moral, practical, communicable and creative activity. *J Adv Nurs* **13**(4): 462–67

Smith BA (1998) The problem drinker's lived experience of suffering: an exploration using hermeneutic phenomenology. *J Adv Nurs* **27**: 213–22

UK Alcohol Forum (2001) *Guidelines for the Management of Alcohol Problems in Primary Care and General Psychiatry.* Tangent Medical Education, High Wycombe

7

Action stage: Nursing those patients who want to control their drinking

This chapter will outline the principles involved in working with patients who are aiming to change their drinking pattern from either abstinence (i.e. following a planned period of sobriety) or directly from chaotic problematic drinking. It will give practical advice on how to implement such a programme, with case studies of patients nursed using humanistic nursing skills.

At the end of this chapter, the reader will:

- Have an deeper understanding of some of the tools used with controlled drinking, such as drinking diaries, time-flow charts
- Have a further understanding of the action stage of change
- Be reflecting on some issues relating to women's services.

As has already been said, the action stage is marked by the patient having made a decision, having planned for change, and is now starting to implement the change process. Buxton *et al* (1996) describe their decisional balance being heavily weighted in favour of change, and the goal of the nurse is to help the patient to maintain that commitment to the process, using reinforcement management and the helping relationship (Burbank *et al*, 2000). Reinforcement management refers to the nurse encouraging patients to record their drinking using the tools and diaries that they have developed together; this has the effect of helping patients to continue with their progress, as there is an inherent sense of self-reward operant in this process.

Controlled drinking as a concept has come to fruition over recent years. Anthenelli and Schuckit describe this as a clinical milestone, while at the same time advise patients that abstinence is the most relevant goal of treatment for those with alcohol dependence. This is based on the work of Schuckit who suggests that a) few alcoholics are likely to achieve a prolonged period of moderate drinking; b) there is an inherent difficulty in predicting who will be successful; and c) the natural course of alcohol dependency is marked by periods of relatively moderate drinking followed by a worsening of problems. However, Velleman (1992) argues that there is overwhelming evidence to show that some people with serious problems are able to return to controlled drinking. Certainly, Heather and Robertson (1981) and Sobell and Sobell (1978) describe how previously severely dependent problem-drinkers can continue at drastically reduced levels following treatment. Moreover, the research findings on controlled drinking (Heather and Robertson, 1981) have precipitated a more dynamic, flexible approach to treatment, and Wangaratne *et al* (1990) argue that this approach helps us to individualise care.

This in itself is consistent with humanistic nursing principles, which view human beings as unique and incarnate beings. The first patient we meet in the following case study had tried controlled drinking in the past, but his drinking was again out of control. He had not attended any follow-up support on discharge from a residential rehabilitation programme, a fact which he now bitterly regrets, as he did feel he had progressed well in the unit. When he was re-referred to the unit seven months after discharge as an outpatient, the decision was to offer him abstinence-based treatment, as there is evidence to suggest that controlled drinking is not appropriate for those who have failed in the past (Ward, 1988). However, when the charge nurse completed an individual assessment, he felt it more appropriate to stay within what the patient was asking, as there was a genuine risk he would opt out of treatment. The charge nurse was aware that there was risk inherent in working against what the evidence suggested. For him the issue was more the fact that the patient had a clear idea of what had gone wrong; moreover, he believed it important to stay within his patient's frame of reference despite his chaotic recent past. This is supported by Paterson and Zderad (1988) who suggest that a nurse has to 'accept and believe the chaos of existence as lived and experienced by each man…'

* * * * *

Case Study 11

Mike is a 29-year-old insurance broker who works long hours and travels throughout England visiting clients. He has been a heavy drinker since he was 18, and describes drinking out of control over a period of five years. The problems he faced when he was first referred last year for his initial treatment programme included emotional difficulties (irritability, low mood), financial problems (credit card debt that he was ignoring), and relationship difficulties (his new wife had threatened to leave within six months of marriage because he had not kept his pre-wedding promise of reducing his consumption).

After completing an inpatient rehabilitation programme over a period of six weeks, he opted for controlled drinking, but did not come back for follow-up because of work commitments. His drinking soon rose from a planned 22 units per week to something in the region of 50–70. Although he claims to have no signs of withdrawal, he does admit to experiencing cravings, and to lying to his wife about when he has been drinking.

This time Mike identifies his problems as being much the same as the last presentation, but although he no longer has the financial problem, he has an added problem: he is on a warning from work because he smelled of whisky when he visited a client. He is now office-based on probation, and feels he was lucky not to have lost his driving license, as the one occasion he was breathalysed he was just under the legal limit. Although he is motivated to change his drinking, and had re-read his action folder from the previous admission prior to his appointment as a refresher, he does seem a little low in mood.

The charge nurse assessed Mike to be in the action stage of change, as evidenced by the positive statements and the planning that Mike had taken in anticipation for the re-referral. He was concerned that Mike might have an element of clinical depression, because he reported a general loss of interest at home, poor concentration, disturbed sleep and appetite, and some irritability and agitation. However, all these symptoms could be attributed to his increased alcohol consumption. As a precaution, the charge nurse helped Mike to complete a Beck depression inventory based on Beck *et al* (1961), which was completed and scored as follows:

BECK DEPRESSION INVENTORY					
Name: MIKE		Date:		Scored by: CHARGE NURSE	
On this questionnaire, there are groups of statements. Please read each carefully, then pick one statement from each group that best describes the way you have been feeling FOR THE PAST WEEK (INCLUDING TODAY). Circle the number beside the statement, and if more than one applies, circle each one that does. Be sure to read all the statements before you make your choice.					
A)	I do not feel sad	0	B)	I am not particularly discouraged about the future	0
	I feel sad	1✓		I feel discouraged about the future	1✓
	I am sad all the time and can't snap out of it	2		I feel I have nothing to look forward to	2
	I am so sad or unhappy I can't stand it	3		I feel that the future is hopeless	3
C)	I do not feel like a failure	0	D)	I get as much satisfaction out of things as I used to	0
	I feel I have failed more than the average person	1✓		I don't enjoy things the way I used to	1✓
	As I look back on life, all I can see is a lot of failures	2		I don't get real satisfaction out of anything any more	2
	I feel I am a complete failure as a person	3		I am dissatisfied or bored with everything	3
E)	I don't feel particularly guilty	0	F)	I don't feel I am being punished	0✓
	I feel guilty a good part of the time	1		I feel I may be punished	1
	I feel quite guilty most of the time	2		I expect to be punished	2
	I feel guilty all of the time	3✓		I feel I am being punished	3
G)	I don't feel disappointed in myself	0	H)	I don't feel I am any worse than anyone else	0
	I am disappointed in myself	1		I am critical of myself for my weakness or mistakes	1✓
	I am disgusted with myself	2✓		I blame myself all the time for my faults	2
	I hate myself	3		I blame myself for everything bad	3
I)	I don't have thoughts of killing myself	0✓	J)	I don't cry any more than usual	0✓
	I have these thoughts but would not carry them out	1		I cry more than I used to	1
	I would like to kill myself	2		I cry all the time	2
	I would kill myself it I had the chance	3		I used to cry but now I can't even though I want to	3
K)	I am no more irritated now than I ever am	0	L)	I have not lost interest in other people	0
	I get annoyed or irritated more easily than I used to	1✓		I am less interested in other people than I used to be	1✓
	I feel irritated all of the time	2		I have lost most of my interest in others	2
	I don't get irritated anymore, I just can't	3		I have lost all of my interest in others	3

BECK DEPRESSION INVENTORY					
M)	I make decisions as well as ever	0	N)	I don't feel I look any worse than I used to	0✓
	I put off making decisions more than I used to	1✓		I am worried that I am looking old or unattractive	1
	I have greater difficulty making decisions	2		I feel there are permanent changes in my appearance that make me look unattractive	2
	I can't make decisions anymore	3		I believe I look ugly	3
O)	I can work about as well as before	0	P)	I can sleep as well as I used to	0
	It takes an extra effort to get started	1		I don't sleep as well as I used to	1
	I have to push myself very hard to do anything	2✓		I wake up 1–2 hours earlier than usual and find it hard to get back to sleep	2✓
	I can't do any work anymore	3		I wake up several hours earlier than I used to and cannot get back to sleep	3
Q)	I don't get more tired than usual	0	R)	My appetite is no worse than usual	0
	I get tired more easily than I used to	1✓		My appetite is not as good as it used to be	1✓
	I get tired from doing almost anything	2		My appetite is much worse now	2
	I am too tired to do anything	3		I have no appetite anymore	3
S)	I haven't lost much weight, if any, lately	0✓	T)	I am no more worried about my physical health than usual	0
	I have lost more than 5 pounds	1		I am worried about physical problems, such as aches and pains, constipation	1✓
	I have lost more than 10 pounds	2		I am very worried about physical problems and it's hard to think of much else	2
	I have lost more than 15 pounds	3		I am so worried about my physical problems that I cannot think of anything else	3
	I am purposely trying to lose weight by not eating		Yes/No		
U)	I have not noticed any recent change in my interest in sex	0	NOTES FOR THE ASSESSOR TO FILL IN AFTER THE PATIENT HAS COMPLETED THE FORM. *Score* = 22/63 *Signed*: C/N		
	I am less interested in sex than I used to be	1✓			
	I am much less interested in sex	2			
	I have lost interest in sex completely	3			

Figure 7.1: Beck's Depression Inventory

When the charge nurse had scored the sheet, he discussed some of the individual items with Mike. During their session, Mike was able to say that the majority of the items where he scored significantly (e.g. feelings of disgust, irritability, guilt) would change if he had reduced his drinking again. He was concerned about the sleep pattern, but agreed to use a relaxation tape (provided by the charge nurse) in the evening, and use some practical sleep management tips, such as not drinking caffeine in the evening, having a bath with lavender before he went to bed. Mike also mentioned to the charge nurse that there were times when he was drinking almost a bottle of whisky a day, and he was concerned that he may have damaged his liver. The charge nurse also helped Mike to complete another decision chart to re-affirm his commitment to change. This is Mike's interim care plan as negotiated between himself and the charge nurse. It covers the first week of his new controlled drinking programme:

Date: 00/00

Stage of change: Action

Level of intervention: Substance

Phase of the nurse-patient relationship: Identification

Partners in Mike's care: *Mike, wife, charge nurse, unit doctor*

Objective: For Mike to establish a week of drinking 3 units a day on 5 days and 2 days abstinent

CARE PLAN:

1)   Mike will use a new drinking diary.

2)   Mike will follow the programme in his new action pack as planned on 00/00 by himself and the charge nurse, and attached.

3)   Mike will keep a mood diary of the week ahead to track any changes in how he is feeling.

4)   Mike will follow a bedtime-routine to try and establish a baseline sleeping pattern. This will involve in particular: no coffee after 6pm; a relaxation routine using the tape provided by the charge nurse; a milky drink at night.

5)   Mike will invite his wife along to join him for part of the next session.

6)   The charge nurse will discuss Mike's Beck's Inventory result with the unit doctor, and feedback any further advice to Mike next week.

7)   The charge nurse will arrange for a blood test to be taken next week to check Mike's liver enzymes; they have not been measured for almost a year and he is concerned that there may be damage.

Date for review:

Signed: *Mike*   Signed: *CN*

Figure 7:2 Care plan: Action

This care plan outlines several points that emerged from the session with Mike. Particular mention is made of an 'action pack'. This is a tool box for patients undergoing a controlled drinking programme. Each patient is helped to collate a folder of information, which they will find useful in helping them to maintain their levels of motivation during the period of change and during the ensuing maintenance stage. It contains as standard a section for copies of their care plan, but also has several items that are individualised for each patient's unique requirements. In Mike's case it contained the following, some of which are discussed in detail at the end of the list:

- Care plan and appointment card
- Drinking diary
- Decision chart
- Goal and reward sheet
- Target chart

- Tips and reminders
- Mood diary
- Resource diary
- Sleep chart

The care plan that was included is seen in *Figure 7.2* (*Page 86*); as the action folder is ring bound, each week when he is seen by the charge nurse, Mike will help to evaluate it and add the new one. The top copy will remain in his case-notes, but Mike will have a photocopy. Using Peplau's model of care, this style of working incorporates the openness and frankness that is associated with the nursing alliance. Mike is an active partner in his own care, and with the charge nurse adopting a client-centred approach within a humanistic framework, he is helped in a way that encourages growth and forward movement. It demonstrates that nursing is an educative instrument (Peplau, 1988).

Drinking diary

This is a standard tool as seen in previous chapters, and as provided in *Chapter 10*. Mike planned some specific goals for his drinking—he decides to drink no more than three units of alcohol a day and have two alcohol-free days. This is eight units less than his previous attempt, but Mike has chosen this target himself as he believes that the four units a day he was having, with no alcohol free days, were enough to trigger cravings and make him think 'just one more'. With this diary, he has a goal and reward sheet, and a target plotter. This is a copy of each:

Mike's Goals for week commencing 00/00:
I will drink no more than 3 units a day on 'drinking days'
I will not drink on Sunday or Wednesday
I will drink the units after work, in safe company

Specifics:
I will drink pub measures of single malt with water on my way home from work. I will eat a meal when I get home with my wife, who will join me in the pub for two of the evenings (on the days when she does not work) before we eat. My two alcohol-free evenings will also be with my wife, as she is not working then.

Rewards:
If I achieve this, I will have saved enough money for 2 music CDs, and I will buy them before my next appointment.

MIKE'S TARGET CHART						
More						
20						
19						
18						
17						
16						
15						
14						
Less						
units / week	1	2	3	4	5	6

Figure 7.3: Goals, specifics, rewards and targets

As can be seen, there is scope for marking above and below the target areas. This is merely acknowledging that things do not always go to plan. The sheet has been made out this way because, should Mike drink more (or less) than he planned, then no emphasis will be placed on his 'failure' to achieve targets, especially as, if he fills in the diary accurately, the specifics will be recorded anyway.

The tips and reminders are a list of useful pieces of advice that help patients to cope with their programme and with the actual drinking in a safe way. The list that Mike has is taken from his previous programme, which he completed on a group basis and decided to re-use. It is based on the work of Ward (1988), but a similar list can be found in Velleman (1992):

Before I drink I will make sure I have eaten during the day, and make sure that I do not have a lot of money in my wallet. I will leave my credit cards in a safe place so that I am not tempted to draw out more money for drinking.

When I do drink, I will drink slowly, dilute my whisky with water, and will not mix my drinks. I will only drink in one pub (where my friend is the landlord and knows I am trying to reduce my drinking), and I will sit at a table away from the bar. I will not join in with rounds with my colleagues, whom I have told about my difficulty. I will have one game of pool before I leave, because I find it unwinds me after work and I feel less irritable. It also keeps me away from the 'drinkers'.

The sleep chart and resource file are both included at the end of the book in the resource file, and basically offer advice and monitoring of his sleep pattern, and useful telephone numbers should he feel at risk of drinking.

The mood chart is a diary that helps Mike to understand when he has difficulties, and will help the charge nurse to assess his mood when read in conjunction with the Beck's inventory. Here is one example:

Date and Time	What were the circumstances, e.g. Who was I with? Where?	How did my mood change? Describe	Did anything make me feel better?

Figure 7.4: Mood Chart

Mood Chart

Figure 7.4 (*Page 90*) is a diary to help you to understand how your mood fluctuates—either on a daily basis, weekly basis, or for some people on an hourly basis. The intention is for you to fill it in as best you can, highlighting what for you are the key issues. Please bring it back with you to each session, as we can then explore it together.

* * * * *

When the charge nurse reflected on his practice with the author (acting as clinical supervisor), this is what he said of nursing Mike for the second time:

CN: *When Mike was re-referred, I was a little disappointed. I felt I had somehow let him down by not encouraging him enough to return to the support groups. I wondered what could we as a team have done to prevent this from happening. I even had a look at some of the stuff by Heather and Robertson (1981) in the unit library, because I wondered if we needed to update anything. It wasn't as if he was a special case or anything, because sure, many folk go away and relapse, but I think I related strongly with him because he is in the same age, was married about the same time as me, and we support the same football team! I realised when we met up that he had made some poor choices, and hey, don't we all at times?*

More than that though, I realised that both he and I wanted a quick fix—I wanted to offer another inpatient stay straight away because I knew that much of the evidence pointed to that being a fast solution. He wanted to drink normally, turn the clock back and not be in trouble with his boss. I held onto that thought as it occurred, decided to stay in his frame of reference, and built up a programme with Mike that addressed both of our concerns. It's about meeting each other on common ground, being creative—it's why I came into nursing I suppose.

Schön (1983) talks of reflecting in and on practice and says our knowing is in our action. The charge nurse demonstrated both in his reflections, as he described going away and looking at the unit's learning resources (reflecting on practice), and at the same time his perception of the dynamics within the session (wanting a quick fix) demonstrates reflection in action. He is also demonstrating part of what has become the third premise of the Tyneside Group (Barker *et al*, 1997), namely that '…nursing involves caring with rather than caring for people, irrespective of context of care.'

It is worth noting at this point that Mike had asked to bring his wife along for part of the next session. Couple counselling is offered in many areas, but the unit's philosophy is to offer patients the option of bringing their partners along for part of a session if they should so wish. It is not couple counselling; there are marriage guidance agencies, and often the local councils on alcohol offer this service. Instead, it is not only an acknowledgement that family therapy and marriage work is a specialist service in itself, but it is also an acknowledgment of the nursing alliance. Peplau (1988) describes how roles are important within the nurse-patient relationship and talks of the educative function of nursing. This must extend wherever the patients wish it to carers and their families for them to be included as part of the alliance. When someone is on detoxification, for instance, or indeed a controlled drinking programme, families can be a great support.

* * * * *

Case Study 12

Helen is a 40-year-old student psychiatric nurse who had inpatient detoxification last year. She has been abstinent for ten months, attending a women's support group facilitated at a local alcoholism treatment unit one evening a week, as she has requested a women's only support and treatment. She now feels ready to start a controlled drinking programme.

She attended her monthly session with the staff nurse at the local unit, and sounded very positive and determined about her ability to start drinking again. This had been negotiated during her inpatient stay as an option for the future, and the intention was to start it after six months. However, Helen did not see the point then, as she was not going to attend anything special and did not intend to drink alone, so the opportunity for drinking had not arisen. She now has a leaving party to attend and would like to drink 'socially' with her friends without starting a binge.

When Helen attended her session with the staff nurse, she was assessed to be in the action stage of change after a period of being in maintenance. The aim of the session with her key worker was to co-ordinate a successful approach to drinking again. Helen was in quite a different position to the previous patient for several significant reasons. Firstly, she was not in the position of having a spouse or family to support her in change decisions. Helen lived by herself in a small town not far from the college where she was now in her final year. Her parents lived over two hundred miles away and her two teenage children were themselves away at college. So she did not have one of the criteria of successful controlled drinking according to Velleman (1992); namely, having family around her. Secondly, Helen did not want to commence regular, controlled drinking. She wanted to be able to drink on specific occasions, such as at a party, or at a wedding, but not drink the rest of the time. This was related to her present circumstances of living alone and having a limited social life (restricted by both geography and economics). Also, her previous chaotic drinking involved drinking alone at home, a behaviour that she did not feel inclined to repeat just because it was 'part of my programme'.

This session represented a change in her relationship with the staff nurse, who had previously been working with her through the exploitation phase. Then, the emphasis had been on helping Helen to make the most of support resources available, such as the women's group. Now saw a period of re-entry into the identification phase as a whole new set of problems were being processed and a whole new goal was being negotiated. The staff nurse and Helen set about developing an action pack not dissimilar to that produced in the previous case study in terms of actual content, which contained a care plan, drinking diary, decision chart, goal and reward sheet, tips and reminders statement, resource diary and target chart. However, the way that they had been filled in were unique to Helen's situation, and were individualised as they had been produced on the unit's computer.

The care plan that they filled in together is shown in *Figure 7.5*, and demonstrates the difference in their problems:

Date: 00/00

Stage of change: Action

Level of intervention: Substance

Phase of the nurse-patient relationship: Identification

Partner's in Helen's care: *Helen, Women's Group, Staff Nurse*

Objective: For Helen to be able to drink at Anna's leaving party on Friday

CARE PLAN

1) Helen will attend the women's group on Sunday morning this week, in addition to Tuesday night, for extra support and feedback after the party

2) Helen will only drink white wine spritzers[1] for her alcoholic drink, and alternate at a rate of two mineral waters to one spritzer.

3) Helen will take no more than £20 for the night out, £5 of which will be in her make-up bag for her taxi home.

4) Helen will drink no more than five spritzers.

5) Helen will have a meal before she leaves the house.

6) Staff nurse will see Helen in her lunch hour on Monday instead of the usual time, to reduce any wait for feedback.

REVIEW: Monday, 13.00 hrs.

SIGNED: *Helen   Staff Nurse*

Figure 7.5: Helen's Care Plan, Action stage

This care plan was more akin to the tips and reminders sheet that the charge nurse had prepared for Mike in its layout and style; this was not a reflection on how the staff nurse worked, but was more a reflection on how Helen worked. Helen had been attending the closed women's group every week on a Tuesday since she left the unit, and had established a close working relationship with her peers and the group facilitator. It was through that medium that she explored some of her most difficult feelings that had led to her chaotic drinking in the past, such as a traumatic divorce and feeling bullied by her ex husband. The staff nurse was aware of the many complex issues surrounding women and alcohol, and the issues

1   White wine mixed with soda water

surrounding gender-specific service provision for those who prefer it. She wanted her relationship with Helen to be that of one extra support, with the group maintaining its central role in Helen's care; this indeed was Helen's expressed wish. As she said in a reflective practice session:

SN   *I felt a certain degree of anxiety when Helen said that she wanted to drink at the party. Until now, it had been abstinence all the way, with a hint that somewhere on the back burner there was this notion of controlled drinking simmering away, ready for some time in the future. And then suddenly it was here, all in a rush. Only it wasn't. In a rush I mean. She had prepared for this day from the beginning in her head, and shared her thoughts with the group. I was just the one who helped her put it all together. I guess with Peplau's model we expect to be the resource person, the support, the surrogate—it's strange when there is another support that our patients hold as more important really. Our unit's Humanist Philosophy pinned on that wall says it all—that our patients are unique human beings, and that we aim to help them to develop their human potential through the medium of the nurse-patient relationship. That doesn't just mean our one-to-one encounters, however deep and meaningful they may be. That includes every human encounter in the helping environment, and her group features highly.*

* * * * *

A note on women's issues

Helen's case study has once again raised some interesting issues regarding women's service provision. The literature on this is diverse, but many of the conclusions are the same: that women are deterred from entering treatment because of societal double standards about women and drink, that mixed-sex programmes are unsuitable in dealing with some of the more sensitive issues, such as childhood sexual abuse, and barriers to attending include practical factors, such as no crèche facilities (Stewart and Casswell, 1992).

Long and Mullen (1994) found evidence to suggest that women experience difficulty in disclosing personal information within groups, especially male-led groups. However, this is balanced by the findings of Rush (1996) who found that the experience of affiliation with other patients (sober alcoholics, clients), and in particular having a sponsor was essential to achieving sobriety in 82.4% of the members of a cohort of 125 women participants who attended AA. When the unit was considering offering a closed, women only group, this was the type of information gathered alongside patient survey materials on which it based its decision.

Burns (1995) may be stating the obvious when she asserts that women are different from men. What may be less apparent is that when women help-seek for an alcohol problem, they bring along a unique female agenda that necessarily broadens the elements of service provision. For instance, women as child-bearers require links to midwifery services, and liaison nurses employed by trusts may serve to provide that link. Moreover, women face specific social constraints, such as being expected to adhere to given social roles (e.g. carer, mother, worker), and face stigma when using alcohol because they are unable to conform to society's expectations (Coupe, 1991).

When working in a humanist environment, one of the main principles is to care for each patient as an individual. Services therefore have a moral obligation to investigate their provision for women in order to overcome the barriers to help seeking, and offer fully individualised care.

Summary

Throughout this chapter we have seen two distinctly different patient situations, both of which were firmly rooted in the action stage of change. The first highlighted some of the concurrent problems associated with alcohol misuse: depression, relationship difficulties, employment worries. Examples of creative problem-solving were given through the medium of decision-making, planning for drinking, and the supportive dynamics within the nurse-patient relationship. The idea of developing an action pack for these patients has been mooted and demonstrated, giving practical examples of the type of tool to include and its utility for practice. The second demonstrated the unique experience of women who come into our care, and of their unique agenda.

The following chapter will go on to explore what happens after these changes have taken place, in the maintenance stage.

References

Barker PJ, Reynolds W, Stevenson C (1997) The human science base for psychiatric nursing: theory and practice. *J Adv Nurs* **25**: 660–67

Beck AT, Ward CH, Mendelson M, Mock J, Erabough J (1961) An inventory for measuring depression. *Arch Gen Psychiatry* **4**: 561–69

Burbank M, Padula C, Nigg C (2000) Changing health behaviours in older adults. *J Gerontolog Nurs* **26**(3): 26–33.

Burns S (1995) *Improving Women's Access to Alcohol Services*. Alcohol Concern, London

Buxton K, Wyse J, Mercer T (1996) How applicable is the stages of change model to exercise behaviour? *Health Educ J* **55**: 239–57

Coupe J (1991) Why women need their own services. In: Glass IB, ed. *International Handbook of Addiction Behaviour*. Routledge, London

Heather N, Robertson I (1981) *Controlled Drinking*. Methuen, London

Long A, Mullen B (1994) An exploration of women's perceptions of the major factors that contributed to their alcohol abuse. *J Adv Nurs* **19**: 623–39

Peplau HE (1988) *Interpersonal Relations in Nursing*, 2nd edn. Macmillan, Basingstoke

Rush M (1996) Method and design in a study of sober female participants in Alcoholics Anonymous. *J Addict Nurs* **8**(4): 116–20

Schön D (1983) *The Reflective Practitioner: How Professionals Think in Action*. Basic Books, New York

Sobell LC, Sobell MB (1978) Developing a prototype for evaluating alcohol treatment effectiveness. In: Sobell LC, Sobell MB, Ward E, eds. *Evaluating Alcohol and Drug Abuse Treatment Effectiveness: Recent Advances*. Pergamon Press, New York

Stewart L, Casswell S (1992) Treating alcohol problems in New Zealand. In: Klingemann H, Takkala J, Hunt G, eds. *Cure, Care or Control: Alcoholism Treatment in Sixteen Countries*. State University of New York Press, Albany, New York: 131–49

Velleman R (1992) *Counselling for Alcohol Problems*. Sage, London

Wangaratne S, Wallace W, Pullin J, Keaney F, Farmer R (1990) *Relapse Prevention for Addictive Behaviours*. Blackwell Scientific, London

Ward M (1988) *Helping Problem Drinkers—A Practical Guide for the Caring Professions*. Kent Council on Addictions, Canterbury

8
Keeping going: Nursing those who have made the change

This chapter will focus on those patients who have either undergone a detoxification programme and are now looking at ways of remaining sober, or those who are now on a controlled drinking programme and looking at ways of maintaining their change decisions. In other words, it focusses on the maintenance stage of change and relapse prevention. The maintenance stage of change marks the period of time when the patient has successfully made the change he has planned for; however, it does not mean that the story has ended, as we see with Mary:

' I was so pleased when I went home after my detox, but I couldn't believe how anxious I felt as I went through that door! The kids weren't home yet from their pals', and I wanted to cook a special tea for them, me coming home an' all, but it all hit me as I opened the cupboard and I saw where I used to keep the brandy. Part of me just thought for a second 'maybe...' but then I scratched that thought, put the radio on, and started chopping onions. I think the tears were the onions, but maybe it was the relief and the knowledge that I had to still put the effort in, all rolled into one...'

At the end of this chapter the reader will

- Have a greater understanding of the concept of relapse prevention
- Understand some of the tools used, such as a cravings diary.

Some thoughts on the process of relapse prevention

Relapse prevention is the process during which a range of strategies and techniques are adopted to prevent a recurrence of problematic drinking behaviour. It is important to stress that the emphasis is on self-management, so in a nursing setting, the nurse is actively promoting activities that patients will be able to follow through in their daily environment. Using humanistic nursing principles, nurses are able to help patients identify risks to their change decisions, and help them to develop creative, individual approaches to deal with such risks as and when they occur.

Much of the work concerned with relapse prevention stems from the model developed by Marlatt and Gordon (1985) in which the overall goals are to increase awareness of risk, develop effective coping mechanisms, and facilitate lifestyle change. Wanigaratne *et al* define relapse as:

'...a return to previous levels of activity following an attempt to stop or reduce that activity'

(Wanigaratne *et al*, 1990: 9)

This is a useful definition as it covers a return to drinking from abstinence, or to heavy drinking from controlled. It is important to differentiate between lapse and relapse, as those areas that focus on abstinence as the only goal tend to view them as one and the same. In Alcoholics Anonymous, for instance, a common adage is that 'there is no such thing as a slip'. However, if a lapse is treated as a single episode of a reversion to problematic behaviour, then it gives scope for using the episode as a learning tool. Wanigaratne *et al* (1990) argue that treating lapse as relapse encourages patients to allow this to become a self-fulfilling prophecy, by leaving no margin for error.

Relapse is often associated with patients making choices in high-risk situations that are at odds with what they may have planned and practised. Marlatt and Gordon (1985) describe the choices as being between a coping response and a non-coping response, suggesting that when someone is faced with a high risk situation and maintains their resolve, it leads to increased self-efficacy and decreased probability of relapse. The opposite of this would be when a patient chooses a non-coping response that leads to decreased self-efficacy and an increased chance of relapse. High risk situations are entirely individual, as what constitutes a risk to one may well not do so to another, but Cummings *et al* (1980) suggest that risk situations fall into two broad categories: intra-personal determinants (e.g. feeling low, angry, craving or, in some instances, feeling high, confident) and inter-personal determinants (e.g. conflict, peer pressure).

When a person is faced with a high-risk situation, his/her decision whether or not to lapse is influenced by a multitude of factors, and often the antecedents to relapse are rooted in earlier behaviour. Patients with chronic pain who have learned to use alcohol to deal with their pain may face relapse choices if their pain is out of control; for instance, the previous experience may be viewed as positive and 'a quick dram may lead to a quick fix'. Within the confines of the nurse-patient relationship, the opportunity to explore these roots is not necessarily appropriate because of constraints, such as time, training levels of staff, or immediacy of the situation. Counselling has traditionally been an avenue where such issues have been explored, certainly within the community when a patient is on the caseload of the CPN or the district nurse. However, in most nursing settings, it is possible to explore the here and now of their situation and to learn new ways of coping using a range of simple tools, as will be explored further on in this chapter.

Non-coping responses that may lead to relapse are more likely if the patient is experiencing lifestyle imbalance. This may be demonstrated as follows:

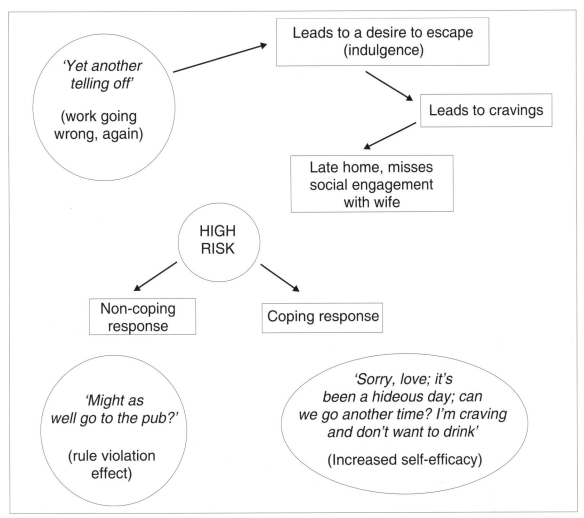

Figure 8.1: To lapse or not to lapse

The following two case studies with reflective discussion are markedly different, but each demonstrates practical approaches to facilitating relapse prevention.

* * * * *

Case Study 13

Joan is a 44-year-old woman who lives in a busy housing estate and has a job that she enjoys at a local factory. She left her husband two years ago, as she felt her problematic drinking was related to the difficulties in her marriage, which included violence within the relationship always associated with her husband drinking. Her two children are both at university, and on their holidays choose to live with their father which causes Joan great distress. Her initial aim when she stopped drinking 18 months ago was for complete abstinence, as she was showing signs of liver damage and felt that she would not want to drink again. She attended Alcoholics Anonymous for a few months, but left because she didn't like the smoking and was unwilling to find a non-smoking group. Joan is pleased that she has a job and what she describes as a nice home, and feels that she has achieved this due to her sobriety and the changes that she has made.

Since then, Joan has met a new partner who drinks heavily. He moved in with her two weeks ago, and two nights ago she was admitted to an orthopaedic ward via Accident and Emergency with facial injuries and a fractured wrist following an episode of domestic violence. Joan had drunk a bottle of vodka after a row, despite managing to remain abstinent since her initial decision to stop drinking, and her partner who had also been drinking had assaulted her.

Her key worker on the ward is the senior staff nurse, who has many years of experience in orthopaedic nursing and who sees this type of admission regularly. She is keen for Joan to have some support on discharge, and has provided her with information on Women's Aid and the domestic abuse helpline, but Joan appears reluctant to look at the leaflets, saying that she didn't need them and she was leaving her partner anyway. She seems more upset about drinking again, and although she does not appear concerned about her injuries, she is worried that she may have damaged her liver again. The staff nurse also felt that Joan was depressed, as she had no appetite, had poor sleep pattern, and was expressing ideas of guilt and worthlessness. However, the staff nurse recognised that these feelings may have been a direct response to the drinking episode.

* * * * *

As can be seen from the above case study, Joan was in the maintenance stage of change. This is evidenced by her prolonged period of abstinence, and is supported by Joan managing to establish herself in the community again following the split, even holding down a job. The staff nurse was concerned that she had relapsed, and wondered if this meant that she was once again in the pre-contemplation stage of change, or even the contemplation. However, if we look back to the earlier discussion of relapse prevention, this fits more into the notion proposed by Cummings *et al* (1980) of lapse, as it was a one-off drink that led to problems, and therefore does not suggest relapse immediately unless Joan continues to use a non-coping response to her current situation. She herself is more upset about drinking than her injuries, which suggests that she continues to have abstinence as her goal.

The orientation and identification phase of the nurse-patient relationship were characterised by the establishment of immediate goals and priorities for starting her physical recovery. Joan had been tearful and reluctant to discuss her situation, but she did make a statement to a police officer and was pressing charges. After the first two days of the admission, when the exploitation phase of the nurse-patient relationship was under way, she did start opening up a little more. Joan's care plan then read as follows (N.B. does not include the care plan relating to her injuries):

Date: 00/00

Stage of change: Maintenance

Phase of the nurse-patient relationship: Exploitation.

Level of intervention: Substance

Partners in Joan's care: *Joan, Staff Nurse, Ward team, Alcohol Problems Clinic*

Objective:　　To help Joan review her change decisions and prevent relapse

　　　　　　To prepare Joan for discharge.

CARE PLAN:

1)　Joan will fill in a new decision chart to re-affirm her decision to stop drinking.

2)　(*Staff Nurse*) will offer Joan some time on Tuesday afternoon to review the situation leading up to the drinking episode.

3)　(*Staff Nurse*) will refer Joan back to the Alcohol Problems Clinic for an initial support and follow up session.

Review date:

Signature:

The following is an excerpt from a supervision session between the staff nurse and her supervisor (the ward sister). It focuses on the staff nurse's discomfort at Joan's reluctance to read the leaflets and talk about her injuries:

* * * * *

Staff Nurse = N; Supervisor = S

N:　*I was so frustrated, I really felt that she needed help, you know, from Women's Aid, but she just didn't want to know.*

S:　Do you think she read the leaflets?

N:　*I don't know. I expect she looked at them later, I hope she did.*

S:　Do you think the violence contributed to the drinking?

N:　*It was odd, really, it was as if the drinking contributed to the violence. I mean, she hadn't been drinking for so long, 18 months, and then after a row she hit the bottle, then bang he hit her.*

S:　Why does that seem odd?

N: *Well, she has such a long history of domestic abuse in her previous marriage, and she only stopped drinking when she got away. This time she has been battered just once, after she drank, and already she is talking about getting away and pressing charges. That seems such a together thing to do, but I felt she wasn't really that together, if you know what I mean.*

S: Was this any different to other situations you have faced?

N: *Yes and no. The difference was her readiness to make a statement, but the similarity was the history—I remember reading Swift's study[1], so I know that many women who drink excessively have a long history of violence towards them. My frustration was really because I really wanted to get her some help straight away, but on reflection, maybe it was better to let it just rest for a while.*

S: Rest for a while?

N: *Yes. I think I wanted my role to be supporter at that point, but she didn't want that. I think she wanted me to be more of a sounding board about her drinking.*

S: Hence the care plan?

N: *That's right. I knew that reviewing what had led up to the relapse is a useful exercise, as is reviewing the commitment to change[2], so I thought that if she could fill in the decision chart here then it would help to strengthen her resolve when she went home. I also felt that a referral back to the clinic would be valuable support after discharge, they would be able to help her with other ways of preventing relapse …*

* * * * *

Within the supervision session the sister was able to encourage the staff nurse to reflect on her actions, and in doing so highlighted some of the learning underpinning her practice. For instance, the knowledge that many women drinkers have a history of domestic abuse and the value of reassessing change decisions.

One useful tool for reassessing decisions is to re-use a decision chart similar to the one used in the contemplation stage of change. However, the wording may be made slightly different to focus on re-asserting previous decisions. This is the chart that Joan filled in:

1   Swift, *et al* (1996)
2   Wanigaratne *et al* (1990).

I made a decision to stop drinking because:	*It made me feel ill, my liver was damaged, I was in debt, and I could not deal with my husband's violence towards me when I was drunk.*
I changed my mind because:	*I was feeling very low, my children never visit me, my partner was drinking and kept encouraging me to join him*
My drinking resulted in:	*I felt more depressed, there was a fight and I had to get admitted to hospital, I am craving again and am worried that I will drink again as soon as I get out.*
What do I want to do now?	*I don't know. I know what I don't want—I don't want to drink, and I don't want to go home to my partner, but I don't know what I do want.*

Figure 8.3: Reaffirming decisions in lapse situations

This is an interesting chart for discussion, because Joan has not made a positive decision. She has stated clearly what she does not want, but has not written what she does want to happen. This may well be due to her low self esteem; she is traumatised by her recent experience with her new partner and it may well have opened up old wounds. Plant (1997) suggests that when people in therapy reflect back on the situation they were previously in when problem drinking, then their feelings become identical in the here and now, even though that experience is in therapy and is, therefore, a supportive environment. The feelings remain the same, hence the potential for relapse is high. With Joan, a similar situation arose, but in reality: there had been arguments in her new relationship and her new partner was a heavy drinker. It would appear that her automatic response was to revert to previous coping mechanisms—albeit in this instance a non-coping response.

Immediate lapse management involved hospitalisation because of Joan's injuries, and immediate nursing care involved maintaining her safety and actively promoting recovery. The nurse found it difficult to engage in a therapeutic nurse-patient relationship because of Joan's initial distress, but that did not stop her from adopting humanistic nursing principles. She acted in an empathic way and offered Joan space and opportunity for talking, which led to creative problem-solving. The nurse's actions in offering Joan time to talk are supported by Smith (1998), who found in a study using hermeneutic phenomenology as its design that telling one's story became an empowering and motivating force.

Joan wrote in her chart that she was experiencing cravings for alcohol. There are several practical strategies for managing cravings, which can be disheartening and de-motivating. Some patients find that distraction is enough. They adopt strategies, such as going for a walk, phoning a friend, going to bed early—often the simple solutions work well. For many, however, a rigorous plan must be in place because cravings may well lead to lapse and possibly relapse, especially when other difficulties are present. Self-monitoring using a craving diary can help both identify triggers and plan for the eventuality of them occurring. Cravings diaries do not need to be complicated, nor do they have to be produced by alcohol specialists. Given the fact that over 50% of weekend evening attendees at A&E departments are likely to have alcohol problems and overall, 1 in 10 of all attendees in Scotland; and also that alcohol problems are currently costing the NHS over £3 billion each year of which £1 billion is spent in Scotland alone (Scottish Executive, 2002), then nurses in general settings are likely to come across patients with alcohol problems on a regular basis. A cravings diary can be included in a resource pack held on the ward along with general leaflets, drinking diaries, resource directories, etc. What is essential is that the nurses are confident in deciding when to give out each component—and cravings diaries fall easily into the remit of relapse prevention in the maintenance stage of change. Here is one example:

Cravings Diary			
Day and approximate time	Circumstances—who was I with, what was I doing, how did I feel when it started	How strong was the craving on a scale of 1 (weak) to 10 (unbearable)	What did I do to make it go away?

Figure 8.4: Cravings diary

Such a diary helps to raise patients' awareness of their cravings as a risk situation, and at the same time can act as a useful tool to open up discussion in one-to-one sessions with their named nurse. The benefit of asking what patients did to make the craving go away is that they are then encouraged to focus on potential solutions. If they say, for instance, that they made a cup of tea then in discussion patients can be reminded to guard against hunger and thirst when out (to avoid going to the pub). If they telephoned a mate to distract themselves, then patients could be encouraged to have a list of names and numbers in their back pocket at all times with change for a payphone. This will help them to develop a resource kit of their own, a tool box for relapse prevention.

* * * * *

Case Study 14

Brian is a 49-year-old businessman who works a 60-hour-week and travels long distances. He started a controlled drinking programme last year, having been threatened with losing his job when he arrived at a meeting smelling of whisky. After a period of four months abstinence and completing an alcohol recovery programme at a local unit, he opted to attend a weekly support group facilitated by an outpatient nurse at the unit. He has never missed a meeting despite his schedule, and had been guaranteed the time to attend by his work as part of their workplace alcohol policy. He appears well, and until this particular incident does not appear to have changed his drinking pattern from his plan.

One evening he attended smelling of alcohol, even though his own rules dictated that on group days his daily allowance of 3 units would be consumed when he got home, with his wife, as part of the evening meal. Another member challenged him, and he said that they had eaten early. The member felt that he was not managing his programme as well as he had been and asked if he needed any further help. Brian declined, and made it clear he did not want to speak in the group. Afterwards, he sought the nurse out, told her that he had been 'economical with the truth', that he had done something, and asked for a one-to-one appointment with her, which was scheduled for a few days later.

As can be see, Brian is also in the maintenance stage of change. Unlike Joan, he is on a controlled drinking programme, therefore his change decision related to a reduction in his consumption. This is a reflective discussion held between the nurse and one of her peers the day after the group, before she had been with Brian in the individual appointment.

* * * * *

N = Nurse; P = Peer

N: *I though he looked edgy when he first came in, but I wasn't sure.*

P: Edgy?

N: *Aye, he seemed uncomfortable when folk were having a cup of tea at the start, and not as chatty as usual. I didn't get a chance to chat to him myself, but as soon as he sat down I knew something was wrong.*

P: What did you think it was?

N: *Well, I thought he'd taken a dram. Brian always has his 21 units a week, never ever misses one, it's become like an obsession with him. I thought that's why he was uncomfortable.*

P: How do you mean?

N: *Well, I thought that he had taken more, and the fact that this was not what he had planned made him edgy.*

P: And is it a disaster? Do you think he drank more, not just that he drank earlier, so is this a disaster?

N: *Och, no, it's only a disaster if this carries on. To be honest, I felt that he didnae want to talk in the group because he had something he didn't want the others to know. Hopefully by tomorrow he'll be able to tell me, then we can deal with it. I find that folk telling lies either openly or by omission are doing so to protect themselves from facing their problems. So long as I can help him feel that whatever has happened it is not a disaster, and it can be overcome and dealt with, then he's going to feel a bit better about it.*

P: I'm interested that in the group it was another member who challenged him and not you.

N: *Well, he did it in a really supportive way, and it seemed important to let the members deal with it themselves. He said something at first like 'You told us that you drink later on Tuesdays, after the group, but I can smell alcohol now'. I felt that this was acceptable confrontation, a process comment really; there was no value judgement, no personal attack. Brian could accept it or reject it. He thought about it, then answered, and even though what he said probably wasn't true he didn't need to dig himself in any deeper.*

P: How will you approach things tomorrow, do you think?

N: *I want to let him know that whatever has happened, it is not a disaster, and that I understand why he was uncomfortable with not telling the truth. Velleman[3] suggests that folk lie because they either feel the consequences of telling the truth might not be in their interest, or because they are trying to deny to themselves what has happened, or because they are trying to boost their self esteem. I won't know until tomorrow, but I will try to put myself in his shoes so that I can understand a little better.*

* * * * *

Once again, this situation is unusual in that the nurse does not know what problems have developed for Brian because they have not yet met for his key worker session. However, he has told her and the group that his drinking pattern has changed, even if only for that particular day, and he has asked for help quickly. The staff nurse was able to discuss some of the issues in the reflective practice session and, in particular, was able to highlight her use of empathy as a humanistic nursing skill to aid her understanding of his situation. She also shared her knowledge with her peer of a model that suggests reasons why people with alcohol problems lie.

When Brian arrives for his one to one session, the nurse has a variety of approaches to help him share his problems. Importantly, Paterson and Zderad (1988) suggest that a nurse has to accept and believe in *'the chaos as existence as lived and experienced by each man despite the shadows he casts, interpreted as poise, control, order and joy'*. Adopting this key assumption of humanistic nursing will allow her to help Brian move on. Velleman (1992) suggests that when a (client) patient misattributes a situation, it is up to the (counsellor) nurse to a) understand the world from his viewpoint; b) let him know she is going to take the time to listen; and c) reassure the (client) patient that nothing negative will happen. This was written for a counselling situation and is easily adaptable for nursing. However, point c) needs careful scrutiny before being accepted unconditionally. Velleman himself acknowledges here that sometimes the (client) patient needs to be gently confronted. One nursing situation where this may well be relevant is if a patient has been drinking on the ward where he/she has agreed as part of the treatment programme that he/she would not. This will in many instances lead to automatic discharge. It does not mean, however, that the service wipes its hands of the patient, and in these situations something positive should always be arranged. For instance, he may be able to be transferred to a detoxification unit with a Designated Place until being reassessed the next day. A Designated Place is one set up, often as a provision of the Mental Health Act, where patients who are intoxicated are able to be admitted and

3   Velleman (1992: 126)

observed overnight prior to entering into a detoxification programme or some other support mechanism. It could be that the patient returns home before coming back to see the staff the next day, or he/she contacts Alcoholics Anonymous, for instance. As part of relapse prevention, such contingencies are discussed in advance by the nurse and patient as a crisis management plan for lapse.

Marlatt and Gordon (1985) developed their discussion of lapse and relapse further by talking about a second stage of relapse in which people decide to carry on drinking after starting. They propose that this stage has four phases, or steps:

1. Stress or anxiety, because the patient has broken his no drink rule (or change decision), leading to;

2. self blame leading to;

3. drinking more to reduce the stress and self blame, leading to

4. the perceived positive benefits of alcohol prolonging the drinking episode.

If this is applied to Brian's situation as we know it to be, then the only phase apparent would be the first because he told the group that he had acted in a way other than that planned by drinking earlier in the evening. The nurse will not find out if he has reached phase 2, 3 or 4 until they spend some time together in a one-to-one session. However, during the treatment programme that he undertook previously, Brian learned some anxiety management techniques. One of the themes of nursing care in Peplau's model (1988) is anxiety as a function of the human experience and of the experience of being ill. There is an acceptance within the model that anxiety will be experienced by the nurse as well as the patient and is, in a way, a function of the nurse-patient relationship. If the nurse is able, therefore, to help the patient accept his anxiety as a normal function of the human condition, then he will be able to move on to find creative solutions to resolve it.

Whatever the setting, the nurse can encourage Brian to look on the alteration from his change decisions as a lapse and not a relapse. He can be encouraged to look at the coping skills that he has developed and identify what changed, or what was happening in his life that led him to not utilise them. This could be done in a simple brainstorm, or a simple diary, or something more structured, such as the following:

Problem Situation (What seems to be going wrong?)	*I am working long hours again, and having my planned drinks earlier; I have also drunk more than I wanted to three times this week.*
Planned Contingency (What I planned to do if this occurred)	*I planned to talk to my wife, or phone up the unit.*
Actual actions (What I did about it instead)	*I hid, didn't tell anyone.*
Outcome (What happened when I carried out the actions above)	*I went into myself, introverted, stopped talking to my wife, then we had a row so I drank a bit more again.*
Do I need to re-negotiate my plans (Is controlled drinking still the best way forward?)?	*I still think I can manage because I have done so for a long time now. But I believe there has to be some changes—I need more support at home to succeed, and I need to look at my excessive work commitments. I also need to remind myself that it is a day at a time and not look too far ahead.*

Summary

In this chapter we have seen some of the skills associated with helping our patients to maintain their change decisions. Both of these patients have faced a lapse situation and asked for help immediately; this reminds us that lapse does not mean relapse. Further examples of some of the exercises that patients may find useful are to be found in *Chapter 10*.

It is worth helping our patients to organise their charts, tables, plans, quizzes, and other exercises in a folder similar to the action pack of the previous two chapters, because most people find them a useful reference in later months.

The next chapter looks very specifically at the role of the nurse in relation to medication and other supports.

References

Cummings C, Gordon J, Marlatt GA (1980) Relapse: prevention and prediction. In: Miller WR, ed. *The Addictive Behaviours*. Pergamon, New York: 291–321

Marlatt GA, Gordon JR (1985) *Relapse Prevention: Maintenance Strategies in the Treatment of Addictive Behaviours*. Guildford Press, New York

Peplau HE (1988) *Interpersonal Relations in Nursing*, 2nd edn. Macmillan, Basingstoke

Plant M (1997) *Women and Alcohol—Contemporary and Historical Perspectives*. Free Association Books, London

Scottish Executive (2002) *Plan for Action on Alcohol Problems*. Scottish Executive, Edinburgh

Smith B (1998) The problem drinker's lived experience of suffering: an exploration using hermeneutic phenomenology. *J Adv Nurs* **27**: 213–22

Swift W, Copeland J, Hall W (1996) Characteristics of women with alcohol and other drug problems: findings of an Australian survey. *Addiction* **91**(8): 1141–50

Velleman R (1992) *Counselling for Alcohol Problems*. Sage, London

Wanigaratne S, Wallace W, Pullin J, Keaney F, Farmer R (1990) *Relapse Prevention for Addictive Behaviours*. Blackwell, Oxford

9
Help from other sources: The nurse's role

This chapter will discuss issues surrounding medication, different sources of professional help, and self help groups.

After reading this, the reader will have a greater understanding of:

- Pharmacological treatment of alcohol problems
- Where nursing fits in with alternative approaches, in particular Alcoholics Anonymous
- Partnership working with other disciplines and agencies.

Importantly, what will be demonstrated is the maintenance and furthering of nursing's unique role and function within a humanistic framework, while at the same time achieving the principles of partnership.

There is no doubt that medication will at some stage feature in the patient's pathway to change. In the action stage, for instance, if the patient is undergoing detoxification, as we saw in *Chapter 6*, he is likely to be prescribed a reducing regime of a benzodiazepine. In the maintenance stage of change, it is possible that a drug, such as acamprosate, will be prescribed as an adjunct to counselling with the overall aim of relapse prevention. There are circumstances where it may be appropriate for an aversion agent, such as disulfiram, to be prescribed. In all such cases, the nurse's role is clear: to provide support and information on the use of the drug and to monitor the effect, be this in an inpatient setting or in the community. This section will now discuss some of the most common drug therapies and outline the evidence-base for their continued place in the toolbox.

Acamprosate

This drug was developed in the 1980s after it was found to prevent relapse of drinking behaviour in alcohol-dependent patients in 14 out of 16 trials. These were conducted as placebo-controlled, double-blind clinical trials that were parallelled and randomised (Mann and Koob, 2001; Mason and Ownby, 2000). Garbutt *et al* (1999) largely supported these findings and suggested that it appears to reduce drinking frequency, although they were unable to draw any specific information from data sources that measured its effects on enhancing abstinence or reducing time to first drink (after a period of abstinence in previously chaotic drinkers).

It is thought to act on the central nervous system by reducing or inhibiting cravings, and by inhibiting neurotransmitter systems; thereby, it is thought to reduce alcohol consumption. In other words, it appears to act on brain bio-mechanisms that are involved in perpetuating alcohol dependence.

If a patient is to be prescribed acamprosate, there are common questions that tend to be asked, and in many circumstances the nurse is in a position where she is expected to be the resource person. The drug company who currently market acamprosate have produced patient information literature that is always distributed with the prescription. The following is a list of typical questions asked, with the sort of answers that have been found helpful in the author's patient groups:

Q: *Does this drug have any side effects?*

A: In some patients it causes a stomach upset for a few days. This is not usually sickness, just a vague queasiness that usually passes after two or three days. Some patients have had diarrhoea. What we have said here is that, if this persists, we will stop the prescription if it is intolerable. Rarely, people have reported a rash, and even more rarely people have had a worsening of their depression. Should you have any worries, please do not hesitate to ask.

Q: *What if I drink? Will I be ill?*

A: No: this drug is not the type of antagonist that makes someone ill if they drink.

Q: *How long will I have to take it?*

A: All the research says that if you are comfortable on it, have no side effects, then up to one year. It is not instead of the support you are getting here, it is in addition to it.

Q: *Will this help me to detox?*

A: No. This is not a detox drug, but we like to start it as soon as possible if you are going to have it, so it may well be started during your detox.

Disulfiram

This is a drug that inhibits an enzyme known as aldehyde dehydrogenase, which has the effect of raising the levels of acetaldehyde in the bloodstream if a patient drinks alcohol. When this happens, a variety of unpleasant effects are triggered, such as hypotension, nausea, flushing, and a red rash. It therefore functions as a deterrent to people who are prescribed it, as fear of these symptoms is often enough to prevent alcohol consumption. Garbutt *et al* (1999) reviewed the evidence-base for its efficacy, and found the following:

- The literature is substantial, but there are limited controlled clinical trials (11 out of 135 studies)

- There is modest evidence to suggest that disulfiram reduces drinking frequencies (oral disulfiram)

- Where administration is supervised, subjects had significantly improved outcomes in drinking frequency

- Disulfiram implants, which are surgically implanted, were not demonstrated to have any benefits over oral; indeed, the studies were inconsistent.

The usual starting dose is a loading dose of 400mg, dropping on day two to 200mg a day. Again, the drug company that markets disulfiram provide patient information literature and a warning card to be carried around with the patient, but these are typical of the questions that patients ask:

Q: *How long after I have had my last drink should I start the drug?*

A: After 24 hours minimum, but we prefer it to be two days.

Q: *What will happen if I drink?*

A: What usually happens first of all is that you get flushing of the face, and you notice your heart beating a little faster. The more you drink, the worse it gets until you feel dizzy. Then you will feel very sick, have diarrhoea, and some people have problems breathing.

Q: *Are there any foods and things that I need to avoid?*

A: Yes. Some pickles and vinegars are safe, but if they have wine or cider vinegar they should be avoided. Use alcohol free deodorants and after shaves: if in doubt do a small patch test. The skin will go red if it is one with alcohol in. Avoid most mouth-washes, but there are some alcohol free ones—ask the local pharmacists.

Q: *Are there any medications I should avoid?*

A: Always tell any doctor you are having treatment from that you are on disulfiram. High dose vitamin C will interfere with its action, and you should not be a blood donor while you are on it. Always ask the pharmacist before buying a cough medicine.

Benzodiazepine medication

This has mainly been covered in *Chapter 6*, where sample regimens have been illustrated to demonstrate the use of diazepam and chlordiazepoxide as detoxification agents in a flow chart and in the symptom severity chart (SSA) charts. They act on the central nervous system and reduce the tremor and other symptoms of alcohol withdrawal and are, therefore, useful in the first few days after an alcohol-dependent patient has stopped drinking.

The SSA chart that is used for monitoring withdrawal symptoms and medication (diazepam) has the following instructions for nursing staff:

1. Before using the score sheet, ensure that the medical staff have signed the form and diazepam is prescribed with the instructions: '2–20 mg as per scoring sheet';

2. Explain to the patient how the form will be used;

3. Take the patient's pulse and write the score in the appropriate box for that date and time;

4. Observe the patient to see if there is any tremor. This can be observed unobtrusively if the patient takes a drink of water with his/her other medication. Again, place the score in the appropriate box;

5. Score the perspiration by feeling the patient's palms while taking his/her pulse;

6. Score anxiety by asking the patient an open question, e.g. 'how are you feeling?'

7. Agitation can be assessed on a continual basis;

8. Formed hallucinations are when a patient can describe them and recognise them as such. Vivid refers to when a patient lacks insight and is acting on them;

9. Initial assessment of orientation should be carried out on admission, and further assessment on a continuous basis, with scoring at medication times;

10. Add the scores and record, then calculate the diazepam as per the key that is provided;

11. Complete the Drug Kardex as normal (inpatient areas), or fill in home-based recording chart.

Remember to review the charts with the GP or unit doctor; if the medication is increasing, or remaining static, the patient must be reviewed by the doctor, and it may be more appropriate to commence a static reduction regime.

Vitamin supplementation

Oral vitamin B complex should be prescribed to all patients undergoing detoxification at a rate of 50mg twice a day for three weeks (UK Alcohol Forum, 2001). Where there is concern about Wernicke-Korsakoff syndrome, then parenteral thiamine should be prescribed (Cook and Thomson, 1997). The role of the nurse is again to act as resource person, and to explain the reasoning behind their prescription. These are typical questions that may be asked:

Q: *Why do I need an injection and 'he' doesn't?*

A: Some people need more than others to prevent a worsening of their symptoms. You fall into that category because your withdrawals are more severe, as you can no doubt tell. Studies have shown that if you swallow a 10mg tablet of this vitamin, you will only absorb 4 or 5 mg of it. If we give you this in injection, you will absorb all 10 mg of it.

Q: *Why do I need vitamin B anyway?*

A: Because people who are alcohol-dependent, or are heavy users, need extra vitamin B during detoxification. The body uses up all its supplies at this time to begin to repair the damage caused by the alcohol on the central nervous system. A healthy body can store 25–30 mg at any time, and uses 1mg a day in normal turnover. Someone with alcohol problems cannot store anything like this amount because of the way alcohol is dealt with by the liver, which has to work a lot harder (increased metabolism), and is often damaged to a greater or lesser extent. If we did not replace it, you would be at risk of complications, such as feeling confused and having a loss of sensation in your legs.

Partnership working in the alcohol field

Patients with an alcohol problem come into contact with treatment services in a variety of ways: they may have been referred by a GP, social worker, courts, family member, district nurse, probation officer, consultant psychiatrist, A&E department, hospital liaison nurse, self—the list is seemingly endless. In Scotland, with the advent of the Executive's Plan for Action on alcohol problems (Scottish Executive, 2002), much of the emphasis is on redesigning services to respond to a whole range problems. Other foci include: providing specialist services for some specific groups, making mainstream services more sensitive, and ensuring that alcohol problems are addressed alongside other health and social problems where necessary.

The need for agencies to work more closely together has been the focus of Government debate (Department of Health, 1994; 1997), with the advent of joint commissioning and joint strategies being the outcome. The Sainsbury Centre (1997) define joint working as the:

'joint activity, primarily, of health and social care agencies in the formulation of strategic policy and the implementation of that policy into local operational activity through the activities of joint planning, provision and commissioning.'

The strategic planning and commissioning of care is not debated in this text; however, within the care planning sections, the reader will see an acknowledgement of the partners in each patient's care. This partnership is built on the immediate individuals and groups with whom patients have care contact during the period of their help-seeking and care receiving. These partners are negotiated between the nurse who is in these settings, his/her primary care worker and the patient; the care plans do not necessarily outline the details of the care that those individuals will be providing, as the focus is on the unique function of the nurse.

Because many of their patients have been involved in a wide variety of helping agencies, it is important for nurses to be aware of and acknowledge the role that these other agencies have performed, or in some instances are still performing for their patients. An open alliance, indeed a co-working relationship between different agents can prevent splitting. Yalom (1985) describes this as a dynamic between individuals in which a patient attempts to split one therapist from another in a co-working situation. So a patient who is also seeing a probation officer as part of a court order may say something like, 'Oh but my CPN says I can drink four pints a night, so long as I don't get into a fight'. If a patient has been referred for shared care between agencies, then joint care planning and shared notes is one effective way of preventing this from happening and is testament to partnership working. Joint appointments, especially at the referral and assessment stage, may also be beneficial.

Such a shared care arrangement can be enriching for the staff as well as the patient, for it gives agencies a chance to share their individual knowledge and expertise. One CPN said this in supervision of a shared care arrangement with a social worker:

'It was really interesting, I don't think she really knew what my role was before, and I certainly didn't know hers. I thought social workers were focussed on money problems and housing problems, but she helped so much with the family counselling. I showed her my care planning tools, and described what the humanist philosophy was all about—she had heard of this in her training, but thought it a woolly, abstract model. Now I've shown her it in action, and she recognises it sits comfortably within her own philosophy of care.'

This type of therapeutic alliance is not, however, appropriate in the same way between some agencies. Alcoholics Anonymous (AA) effectively works alongside the professional agencies, but it is strictly independent of any affiliation with any other organisation (Alcoholics Anonymous, 1989). The organisation has grown from its early beginnings in America in 1935 to become the largest self-help organisation for recovering alcoholics in the world, with literally thousands of groups worldwide. It runs on a 12-step programme aimed at helping its members to live a sober life through essentially spiritual means (Hall, 1991). In the recently published SIGN Guideline 74 (Scottish Intercollegiate Network, 2003), it is recommended that alcohol-dependent patients should be encouraged to attend Alcoholics Anonymous. This is supported by the Health Technology Assessment Report (Health Technology Board for Scotland, 2003) who specifically recommend on page 1–5; para 1.9.7: that 'Introduction to Alcoholics Anonymous and non-statutory agencies…should be part of the overall strategy of specialist NHS services for the prevention of relapse'.

All nurses and all patients have access to the Freephone telephone number in the telephone directory, and any patient wanting to find out more can telephone to find out what is available locally. The organisation does have open meetings and public meetings—public meetings are available for anybody to attend, but to attend an open meeting one must either be a member of AA or the sister organisation Al-Anon Family Groups. In order for us to help patients make an informed choice about where they help-seek, it is recommended that one either attends a public meeting, or asks someone from the local group to come and talk to the staff on the unit; such exchanges provide fruitful discourse and are very enlightening for all concerned.

Hore (1997) advises that anecdotal evidence suggests that individuals who have achieved long term sobriety through treatment programmes followed by self help means develop characteristic behaviour. These he describes as the four Cs:

1. Contact with other sober alcoholics (e.g. attendance at AA);

2. Constructive thinking—'don't take risks';

3. Craving management (cue avoidance);

4. Crisis strategy.

These four Cs can form the basis of discussion in health promotion settings where a known problem-drinker comes into contact with nursing staff, such as the well woman clinic. By encouraging patients to reflect on their self-management strategies, it reinforces their efforts, and acknowledges progress.

Summary

We have seen some of the issues surrounding the use of medication by problem drinkers, and have explored some of the evidence-base pertaining to its efficacy. When nurses are using a humanistic approach to care, they are in an open dialogue with their patients that encourages exploration of the necessity for such prescriptions. Nurses are, therefore, in a position where they are expected to be knowledgeable resources for their patients.

The following chapter explores this resource role further, and adds to the growing stock of tools for use in nurse-patient settings with patients who present with alcohol problems.

References

Alcoholics Anonymous World Services Inc (1989) *Membership Survey*. Alcoholics Anonymous, New York

Cook CC, Thomson ADT (1997) B-Complex vitamins in the prophylaxis and treatment of Wernicke-Korsakoff syndrome. *Br J Hosp Med* **57**: 461–65

Department of Health (1997) *Green Paper: Developing Partnerships in Mental Health*. HMSO, London

Department of Health (1994) *Health of the Nation Mental Illness Key Area Handbook*. HMSO, London

Garbutt JC, West SL, Carey TS, Lohr KN, Crews FT (1999) Pharmacological treatment of alcohol dependence. *JAMA* **261**(14): 1318–25

Hall JM (1991) Recovery in alcoholics anonymous: three nursing theory perspectives. *Perspect Addict Nurs* **2**: 3–6

Health Technology Board for Scotland (2003) *Health Technology Assessment Report 3: Prevention of Relapse in Alcohol Dependence*. NHS Quality Improvement Scotland, Edinburgh

Hore B (1997) Brief interventions are not the panacea. *Alcoholism* **16**(i): MCA, London

Mann KF, Koob GF (2001) *Worldwide Benefits of Acamprosate: Efficacy, Safety, and Quality of Life*. Oxford Scientific Series, Adis International, Chester: 2

Mason BJ, Ownby RL (2000) Acamprosate for the treatment of alcohol dependence: a review of double blind placebo-controlled trials. *CNS Spectrums* **5**(2): 58–69

The Sainsbury Centre for Mental Health (1997) *Together We Stand—Effective Partnerships*. The Sainsbury Centre, London

Scottish Executive (2002) *Plan for Action on Alcohol Problems*. Scottish Executive, Edinburgh

UK Alcohol Forum (2001) *Guidelines for the Management of Alcohol Problems in Primary Care and General Psychiatry*. Tangent Medical Education, High Wycombe

Yalom I (1985) *The Theory and Practice of Group Psychotherapy*. Basic Books, New York

10
Nursing Resource File

Throughout the book various documents and resources have been demonstrated for use with patients at different stages of change and in different clinical settings. This chapter contains samples of some other resources for your reference.

Sleep management handout

Many people have difficulty establishing a normal sleeping routine after they have stopped drinking. This is to be expected, as for sometime your body has effectively been anaesthetised by alcohol, and it needs to re-learn a healthy pattern. Read the enclosed Healthy Sleeping Tips. Make a list of the difficulties you feel you have now with your own sleep pattern:

Now share this list with someone with whom you feel you can talk. Have they had a similar problem? Do you need to re-adjust your list, is there something that you forgot to include?

Chose three of the problems, and rate them on a scale of 1–10, where 1 is the worst it could be, and 10 is the best. For example: *'I lay and think of worries, so can't nod off—this week it is a 3'*.

Sleep Problem Number: **Rating:**

1.

2.

3.

Think of one small thing that you can do to bring each problem up by one point on your scale. For instance, for the above example, you could talk to somebody about the things that are going over in your head, then when you go to bed they are less likely to trouble you as much:

Sleep Problem Number

1.

2.

3.

Put this into practice, and rate your score next week. Repeat this exercise each week, choosing different actions. Use this space to record any thoughts on this with your supporter:

Healthy sleeping tips

Sleeping environment

If you are too hot or cold, or if you go to bed hungry, you are less likely to sleep well. Likewise, if there is noise, it will interfere with your natural sleep pattern. Try to make sure that you take steps to avoid disturbing your night time comfort. Do you need to wear ear plugs? Is there an intrusive light?

It is important that you only use your bed for sleep, or of course sexual activity (which may help you sleep!)—try not to take your work to bed, for instance, try to avoid watching television in bed, or having major arguments and discussions in bed. That way, you will begin to associate the act of going to bed with sleep, and not with a state of alertness.

Try not to have pets in the bedroom at night, as if they are restless they will wake you.

Sleep pattern

It is important to try and establish a regular pattern of what time you go to bed and what time you wake up. That way, as your period of sobriety settles, or your period of reduced drinking establishes itself as the norm, your body will begin to establish certain norms in its body clock. Persist with this; it will work eventually. Avoid staying in bed until lunchtime, even if you are not at work then. Part of a good sleep pattern is the wind down before bed. Having a warm bath can help to unwind and avoiding caffeinated drinks is important. Try a relaxation routine, or some yoga, or simple stretches to loosen your muscles. Avoid napping during the day, because this will disturb the pattern that you are trying to establish for yourself. It is advisable to avoid nicotine late at night; this stimulates the body to produce adrenaline, which keeps you awake and alert.

Information for patients and their families or friends (home detoxification)

The period of detoxification (known as 'detox'), which is now being planned for you or your relative/friend, has been deemed necessary for several reasons. When anybody has become physically dependent upon alcohol, the process of stopping the alcohol intake causes withdrawal symptoms. These vary in everybody in severity, and can include 'the shakes'; sweats, trembling of the hands, sleeplessness, stomach upsets and, in rare cases, fits. In order to reduce these symptoms to the absolute minimum and to make you feel better, the GP will prescribe some medication to be taken every day, and this will be monitored by the CPN (community psychiatric nurse).

The CPN will visit most days to make sure that the medication is controlling the symptoms and also to make sure that you are all comfortable with the progress of the detox. There are a few things for you all to remember during this time that will make things clearer. The first few are aimed at the person undergoing the detox, but it helps if you all read this.

- Try to take a bath or shower each day in the first few days, as you are likely to sweat more and may become uncomfortable. You may need to change your sheets more often this week—we would hope that your family or friends would be willing to help if necessary

- Try to aim for some tranquillity in the home during this time, as you may find that you are more irritable and sensitive to noise. You are likely to be a little anxious and it is important that your family and friends understand this

- You should not drive while taking the prescribed medication, as you are likely to feel drowsy

- It is important to take a good intake of fluids, as you are likely to be a little dehydrated due to the increased sweating and also to possible nausea/loss of appetite. Try to stick to water or soft drinks and avoid caffeine, which may cause insomnia

- Your sleep pattern will take some time to come back. Many people do not sleep well in the first few days and it is important to have a restful time at home without catnapping, which will prevent you from sleeping at night.

Emergency checklist for supporters during home detoxification in the case of a seizure

Very occasionally, a person who has stopped drinking has an epileptic type fit. When we assessed your friend/relative for home detox, we felt that this was unlikely, but it is not possible to say it will never, ever happen. If your relative or friend has a seizure or fit:

- **Keep Calm**
- Support their head with a pillow, or your hands/forearms
- If possible, turn the person on their side
- Stay until they have stopped shaking and are on their side, then—
- Call the GP as soon as you can safely move to the telephone
- NEVER put anything in their mouth
- NEVER try to restrict their movements or move them to another place unless they are in immediate danger (e.g. the fire)
- IF YOUR FRIEND/RELATIVE IS BLUE IN THE LIPS AND FACE, CALL AN AMBULANCE IMMEDIATELY

Some units or services prefer their patients who are undergoing home detoxification to sign an agreement such as this:

Alcohol Detoxification Agreement

I agree to follow these conditions that have been explained and discussed with both my supporter and I. I understand that the detox may be terminated if I do not comply with the conditions as set out below:

1. I agree to my supporter being involved in a helping capacity during the detox.

2. I agree not to drink alcohol during the detox period.

3. I agree that if I do drink alcohol, I will give my tablets to my supporter who will return them.

4. I agree to be breathalysed on every visit.

5. I will take the tablets as prescribed to me by my doctor, and as advised by my CPN.

6. I agree to attend the appointments on time, and that I will let my CPN know if an emergency crops up and I will not be in.

Signed: ……………………………………………………..

Date …………………..

Witnessed by supporter ………………………………..

CPN involved ……………………………………………….

Drinking Diary

Day	What did I drink?	Where/When/ Who With?	Units	Total (Units and Cost)
Monday				
Tuesday				
Wednesday				
Thursday				
Friday				
Saturday				
Sunday				
Total for week:				

My Personal Drinking Rules:

1.

2.

3.

What will I do if I feel tempted, or if I start craving?

What if I break my rules?

Time	Monday	Tuesday	Wednesday	Thursday	Friday	Saturday	Sunday	Time
12.00am								12.00am
01.00am								01.00am
02.00am								02.00am
03.00am								03.00am
04.00am								04.00am
05.00am								05.00am
06.00am								06.00am
07.00am								07.00am
08.00am								08.00am
09.00am								09.00am
10.00am								10.00am
11.00am								11.00am
12.00pm								12.00pm
01.00pm								01.00pm
02.00pm								02.00pm
03.00pm								03.00pm
04.00pm								04.00pm
05.00pm								05.00pm
06.00pm								06.00pm
07.00pm								07.00pm
08.00pm								08.00pm
09.00pm								09.00pm
10.00pm								10.00pm
11.00pm								11.00pm
Colour Code	SLEEPING		DRINKING		SELF SUPPORT		SOCIALISING	
	EATING		WORKING		RECREATION			

Time-flow chart: Ask the patient to use coloured pencils; 1 week drinking, 1 planned week of abstinence

125

Scoring criteria

PULSE:	
79 or below	0
80-99	1
100-119	2
120 or over	3

TREMOR:	
No Tremor	0
Tremor of outstretched hand	1
Constant tremor of arms	2
Whole body tremor	3

PERSPIRATION:	
None	0
Moist skin	1
Beads of sweat	2
Profuse sweating	3

ANXIETY	
None	0
Understandable anxiety	1
Anxiety and panics	2
Constant panic	3

AGITATION	
None	0
Restlessness	1
Can't remain seated	2
Constantly restless	3

PERCEPTUAL DISTURBANCE	
None	0
Illusion/fleeting hallucination	1
Formed hallucinations	2
Vivid hallucinations	3

ORIENTATION	
Correct	0
Uncertain of date	1
Date wrong more than 2 days	2
Time and place wrong	3

DIAZEPAM

Score	
0-1	No Medication
2-3	2mg
4-5	5mg
6-7	10mg
8-10	15mg
over 10	20mg

Recording chart

	Date								
Time:	8	1	6	10	8	1	6	10	8 1 6 10
Pulse									
Tremor									
Perspiration									
Anxiety									
Agitation									
Perceptual disturbance									
Orientation									
Total									

	Date								
Time	8	1	6	10	8	1	6	10	8 1 6 10
Pulse									
Tremor									
Perspiration									
Anxiety									
Agitation									
Perceptual disturbance									
Orientation									
Total									

Ward	Name:	Unit number:	Consultant:

Index